Transform Your Life

Transform Your Life

Revised and Expanded to Include
How to Have a Flood and Not Drown

Reverend Dr. Barbara King

A PERIGEE BOOK

A Perigee Book
Published by The Berkley Publishing Group
200 Madison Avenue
New York, NY 10016

Copyright © 1995 by Reverend Dr. Barbara King
Book design by Rhea Braunstein
Cover design by James R. Harris
Photograph of the author by Michael Britto

This edition contains the revised text of *Transform Your Life*
(originally published by DeVorss & Co., Inc., copyright © 1989
by Reverend Dr. Barbara King) and the revised text of
How to Have a Flood and Not Drown
(originally published by DeVorss & Co., Inc., copyright © 1990
by Reverend Dr. Barbara King).
The poems "Prayer for Protection" and "I Am There" by James Dillett
Freeman appear by permission of the author.

Biblical quotations appearing in this book are taken from either
the King James Version or the Revised Standard Version.

ISBN: 0-399-51932-7

Printed in the United States of America

This Book
Is Dedicated
to
all the people throughout the world who have given me the
opportunity to be a channel for change in their personal
transformations, and who have
touched me in a special way.
I Love You

Contents

To My Readers

We hear a lot these days about stress and "coping skills." As far as I'm concerned, one of the best jobs of coping with stress was the one Daniel did in the lions' den! I believe in the miracle of Daniel in the lions' den because I've seen what man calls "impossible" become the *possible* with God. But to fully understand this story, we have to go beyond the literal events and look at the symbolism. For instance, image yourself as Daniel. Your den is your mind. When you have thoughts of fear, of worry, of disgust, of hate, of anger, these emotions become the lions of your den.

So what do you do about it? Daniel was known as a man who prayed three times a day. When he was thrown into the lions' den, all he could do was go back to the truths of God. Now perhaps we don't have outer lions, but oh, do we have *inner* ones! They are eating at us, gnawing at us, tearing us apart. At such times, the thing to do is exactly what Daniel did: go to our Father and pray believing the mouths of the lions will be shut. When you go to God about a situation, all the fear and worry *has* to get out of your mind, because, remember, we know scientifically, we know psychologically, that two conflicting ideas cannot occur in the mind at the same time.

The people of Daniel's times were no different from you and me, and neither were their problems. They too wrestled with family relationships, taxes, romantic involvements, self-esteem, money, success in business, war, diseases, poverty, oppression, crime. You name it, they knew it!

Still, through all mankind has or has not done, there has always been a loving, forgiving Father-Mother God. (We say "Father-Mother God" because since everything was created from this one source, then clearly both male and female are contained within It.) And that Father-Mother God has always been just one prayer away. Prayer is all that it takes to shut the mouths of lions; prayer is all that it takes to bring into your heart and mind a cleansing flood that will clear your inner landscape and let you plant new, healthy seeds.

Whatever you are facing, don't let God be the last place you turn. As you will find in the pages of this book, you can save yourself a great deal of time and agony if you turn to God for whatever coping you have to do and seek God first in all things.

Transform Your Life

--- ✳ ---

CHAPTER ONE

What Are You Afraid Of?

Webster defines fear as "an unpleasant, often strong emotion caused by anticipation or awareness of danger." Fear is a very painful emotion, often followed by alarm. When we are fearful, it simply means that we have allowed some object or some other person or some situation to become so large in our consciousness, in the way we see it, in the appearance of it, that we become fearful of it and lose control of ourselves. Then the fear, the thing we dread, seems to be in total command of us. Our lives feel ruined and out of control. But we don't *have* to be afraid. Fear is an emotion, and emotions are ours to control; the emotion does not control us, we are in charge of the emotion.

I have discovered that the best way to work with fear is to get a better understanding of God, a better understanding of who we are in relationship to God, and to work with the Divine plan for our betterment. But many of us are not willing to do this. Just recently I was watching one of the morning talk shows on which a psychiatrist was discussing fear and how it tightens and grips so many people to the point where they have to go in for therapeutic treatment. On this program was a very beautiful young housewife in her early twenties who lived in fear of going anyplace by herself. From the time her husband left for work in the morning, she would not leave her house alone until he returned. Even if they went out to dinner, for some reason she had a phobia of people around them. She was constantly fearful that someone was in the garage or waiting in their home. This fear had such control of her that she had to seek professional help for it.

We Create Fear Where There Was None Before

Most of us aren't so caught up in our fears as was this young housewife. We realize that we can control our fears by looking at them for the nothingness they are and then banish them by speaking the truth about them. The so-called threat we are afraid of, in other words, has no power except the power we give it.

But sometimes we are made fearful by the suggestion that we *should* be afraid. For instance, I read of a man who owned a German shepherd that he had trained to be very fierce and to protect him and his family. When this man was transferred to another city, he gave the dog to a friend of his. A year later he returned and decided to visit his friend. When he reached the friend's house, there was a high fence around the yard and a sign reading "Beware of Dog." On the porch was a dog. Confidently, the man ignored the sign and stepped inside the gate. As he did so, the dog jumped up, roaring and growling, with his hair on end and his teeth bared.

The man said to him, "Now listen, Prince. You know who I am. I'm your first master. I'm the one who brought you here. And I'm *so* happy to see you again!" He kept talking with these beautiful, soothing words of love, and the dog kept growling and rearing up. The man came closer, talking all the while, until finally the dog relaxed and his tail started wagging. At this point, the man approached the dog, petted him, and rang the doorbell.

After the friends had greeted each other warmly, the dog's owner asked in amazement, "But how did you get in the yard?"

"I walked right by Prince," the visitor answered. "I told him who I was, and I came right in."

Even more amazed, his friend said, "You told him who you were?"

"Why yes," the visitor said, "I talked to him and came right to the door."

"But that's not Prince!" the friend said. "Prince died shortly after you gave him to us. We were grieved about it because of our friendship to you, so we immediately purchased another dog who looked just like him. *That* dog, the one you just introduced yourself to, is a killer. We have raised him to protect us. That's why the high fence and the warning sign."

Well, as you can imagine, the visitor was overwhelmed at the thought of what he had just done with this strange dog. He continued his visit, deciding that since he'd gotten past the dog the first time, he could go right back the way he came. But something had happened. As he considered what his friend had said about this dog not being the familiar Prince, it dawned on him that he was afraid. And when he went out and walked past the dog, the dog growled and came to his feet. Rather than responding as confidently as he had done the first time, the man started running, and the dog, of course, chased him. He barely made it to the gate.

Isn't this the story of many of us? We are sometimes at peace about a given situation when suddenly some change in the situation makes us look at it differently. Then our imaginations begin to form pictures of what *could* happen, what *might* happen, what we *expect* to happen (usually the worst). Regardless what our experiences have been up to that point, we let our emotions get involved, and the fear becomes so great in us that we can't see anything else except the object of our fear.

Fear Is Man-Made, Not God-Given

What we need to become convinced of is the words in 2 Timothy, first chapter, verse seven: *"God hath not given us the spirit of fear, but of power, and of love, and of a sound mind."* I take this to mean that we cannot overcome fear with human power, but by the Spirit of the living God that is within us. That's what most of us don't realize. When we call forth the power of this living Spirit within us, we don't have to be fearful.

Here's another example, again involving a dog, to illustrate what I mean. At one time, my household included a French poodle named Ralph. He was extremely friendly and had grown to love all the people who came into the house. One day a mother and her four-year-old daughter came to visit. At the sight of Ralph, the little girl jumped on the couch and screamed in terror. After she had been calmed, I said to the mother, "Are you working with your daughter about her fear of dogs?"

The mother said, "Well, she was bitten by a dog when she was much younger. Now she's scared to death of dogs, and that's that."

"Ah, but it's not that simple!" I answered. "That fear will grow and grow in her conscious thinking until it takes over. Suppose something of utmost importance to her comes up, but it involves passing a dog or being in the presence of one. If you don't begin now to help her work with her fear, she may not be able to rise above it at a crucial moment. And fear, like any emotion, is contagious. If you allow her to continue living with this one fear, to get used to the presence of fear in her mind, it could easily spread to other areas of her life."

And the same holds true for adults. Many of our fears were learned in childhood. We learned to fear the darkness, certain types of disease, poverty; some of us even were taught to fear people who were different from us. Some people never outgrow such fears, which turn into phobias and prejudices and areas of ignorance. But with the right guidance and an awareness of our inner resources, we can *un*learn our fears.

We all know the saying, "Practice makes perfect." When we hear this saying, we might associate it with practicing a musical instrument, for often it was the music teacher from our childhood who reminded us at the end of each lesson, "Practice makes perfect!"

Actually, anything we practice over and over eventually becomes perfected. This includes practicing habits over and over—"bad" habits as well as "good" ones. A child who practices brushing her teeth every morning and night will grow into an adult who automatically reaches for the toothbrush as part of the morning and evening rituals of cleanliness. By the same token, those who practice negative thinking will think negatively when confronted with the strange, the difficult, the challenging. Whatever you practice regularly becomes perfected in your life.

Another saying all students of metaphysics know well is "practice the presence of God." In truth, we know that we are always in the presence of God, for God is. God permeates everything. God forms the basis of everything. God lives and breathes within us all. So we can never be separated from God, though often our circumstances or our level of consciousness may cause us to be unaware of the presence of God.

Thus, when we speak of practicing the presence of God, what we are really talking about is spending time in silent communion with God—listening for inspiration, guidance, comfort, or simply verifying for ourselves that God *is*. Practicing the presence of God, in other words, is making a conscious effort to *know* that God is real, to feel the power of God moving in and through us, our world, and our affairs.

In our early efforts to practice the presence of God, we may not know if indeed we are in the presence of God. Perhaps we are looking for some dramatic change in the environment—a charge in the air, a flash of light, an apparent lifting away from the physical body. All of these experiences may occur. On the other hand, it is equally likely that we will simply feel a supreme sense of well-being, a blessed assurance that whatever we are dealing with, it's all right. It may not look "all right," it may not feel "all right," it may not be called "all right" by anyone else; but somehow, in that blessed, tranquil presence of God, it must be "all right" because there is nothing greater in the universe than the divine being.

This sense of "all rightness" may not come the first time we seek it. We may feel as though our prayers are not being heard. We may wonder if we're praying right or even if prayer is the thing to do in the given circumstances. At such times, it doesn't hurt to keep in mind the wisdom of our elders who understood and were patient with the workings of God. My grandmother, for instance—and probably yours too—used to say, "He may not come when *you* want Him to, but He'll always come on time."

During these periods of waiting, we can fill our minds with uplifting thoughts. Take the Bible in hand and just begin reading wherever the pages fall open. Listen to inspirational music. Re-read a favorite book that revealed answers in the past. Read a daily devotional guide. Attend a religious service or some other kind of spiritually uplifting gathering. Above all, we must continue our prayer work, returning again and again to our own private place of meditation. It is in this private place that we make perfect our ability to feel and know the presence of God.

At the Last Supper, Jesus told the disciples, "Truly, truly, I say to you, he who believes in me will also do the works that I do; and greater works than these will he do, because I go to the Father" (John 14:12). Further, Jesus said, "If you abide in me, and my words abide in you, ask whatever you will, and it shall be done unto you" (John 15:7).

What that says to me is that the miracles Jesus performed are *ours* to perform if we believe and live by His word. We may want our miracles to be on a smaller scale. Instead of raising the dead, we might be satisfied with curing the "incurable" illness. Instead of walking on water, we may simply want the strength to walk into a hostile business meeting and come out surrounded by harmonious goodwill. Instead of feeding 5,000, we may find it enough to feed our family during a time of "paycheck famine."

Think again of Daniel, who was thrown into the lions' den because he would not bow down and worship the king and the idols of his day. Daniel believed in a living God; he kept in constant communion with his God, taking time, three times a day, to pray. So knowing what kind of God he served, he faced the lions with faith. He knew that the God to whom he prayed was a living presence within him, and that It was the *same* Spirit that created the lions.

The next morning the king, who dearly loved Daniel but was simply following the rules of his kingdom when he had Daniel thrown to the lions, went to the den and called Daniel's name. Daniel answered him, saying that God had sent His angels and shut the mouths of the lions. He even praised the king, whom he had served faithfully before his enemies had set the trap that caused him to be thrown to the lions. With the forgiving love and the overcoming power of God in his heart, Daniel said, "O king, live forever" (Daniel 6:21). He had triumphed over a very present and deadly threat.

We Can Do What Daniel Did

All of us have lions in our lives, things that overcome and overwhelm us. But when these lions come upon you, take time to pray, to say, *There is only one power and one presence in my life, God the good omnipotent.* Know that if there seems to be any other power, any other presence, if there is something that is frightening to you, it's because you are giving it the power of your belief, just like our friend who suddenly feared a dog he had so recently petted.

Rather than letting this fear belief control you, speak the word of truth about it. If you have to speak out loud to convince yourself with the fullness of your voice, then do so. If you have to sit quietly and pray about it, do so. Use the power that God has given you. You are created in the spiritual image and likeness with power over everything. Know that the thing that seems to be frightening has no power, no control over you. Know the truth of your being—that God is the only presence; God *is* the only power. And the power is within each of us.

Who's in Control of You?

One of the greatest tests Jesus had to face occurred immediately after He had been baptized by John the Baptist. In the Book of Matthew, we learn that when Jesus emerged from the River Jordan

the heavens were opened and He saw the Spirit of God descending like a dove, and alighting on Him; and lo, a voice from heaven, saying, "This is my beloved Son, with whom I am well pleased" (Matthew 3:16–17).

Then Jesus was led up by the Spirit into the wilderness to be tempted by the devil. And He fasted forty days and forty nights, and afterward He was hungry. And the tempter came and said to Him, "If you are the Son of God, command these stones to become loaves of bread."

But He answered, "It is written, Man shall not live by bread alone, but by every word that proceeds from the mouth of God" (Matthew 4:1–4).

In considering this passage, the first thing we need to understand is that "devil" or "satan" means sense or error consciousness. The *sense consciousness* is that part of ourselves which is concerned first and last with satisfying that which we see, hear, touch, taste, or smell. The sense consciousness has its basis in our thoughts. Unless we are very careful, our thoughts can control us instead of us controlling them.

Thus, when Jesus ended His fast, the sense consciousness of Him was aware that His body desired food. The thought of hunger was uppermost in His mind, and so He was in a position to be tempted by the urge to gratify His senses. "Since you have so much power," the sense consciousness told Jesus, "turn these stones into bread and satisfy that hunger you have after all these days and nights without food."

By this time, though, Jesus had perfected His Christ-self, and He could not be tricked into thinking that bread alone would keep Him alive. He acknowledged the role bread plays in our survival, but more than that, He said that man lives by every word that comes from the mouth of God. In other words, man lives by his conscious awareness of an application of the principles of Truth.

Imagine yourself on an uninhabited island. There is no convenience store around the corner, no fast-food restaurant you can run to for a quick meal, no well-stocked kitchen you can go into and cook a gourmet dinner fit for a king. Just you and the natural abundance of God. Surrounded by all this abundance, but lacking the conveniences we have come to expect as our just due, you have two choices: You can sit there and starve, or you can obey the voice within that says, "Get up and get that banana, that apple. Look around and see what else you can find."

Sometimes we might be tempted to moan and groan about what we don't have, to complain and give up because things are not as we would have them be. But that is not the way of Truth. Truth tells us to be resourceful, to take what we have, bless it, and allow it to fill our needs. You might not have steak in your refrigerator. Maybe all you have in the pantry is a can of pork and beans. But guess what? That can of pork and beans will still fill your stomach and nourish your body. Praise the Lord!

One thing we must never forget is that the words that proceed from the mouth of God are the words of Life itself. There is an inner presence in each of us—the God-self of us—that turns adversity into advantage, lack into abundance, and confusion into order. You can eat all the bread you want, all the steak you can afford. But until you begin to seek spiritual nourishment from the words of Life, your hunger will go unsatisfied. That is why Jesus was able to reject the temptation to turn the stones to bread. He knew that in satisfying His bodily hunger He would still leave unfilled the most basic part of His being.

In the second temptation, the sense or error consciousness of Jesus attempted to flatter Him into thinking that His body was indestructible and that He should throw Himself from the top of the temple to prove His indestructibility. Jesus overcame this temptation by responding, "You shall not tempt the Lord your God" (Matthew 4:7).

In other words, the gift of life is to be used wisely and for good and useful purposes. We know that if we believe in God we shall have life everlasting. Therefore, our task is not to go around testing and questioning the gift of eternal life but to live fully, confident that if we put God first, we shall be guided and protected in all that we do. Knowing this, our primary responsibility is to find ways of pleasing God, not *challenging* God as the sense consciousness would have had Jesus do by jumping off the temple roof.

We sometimes "jump off the temple roof" when what we really need to do is sit in the quiet of the temple and meditate. For instance, have you ever walked off a job at a moment's notice without having made provision for other employment? Have you ever ended a relationship in a fit of anger rather than working to resolve the problem? Have you ever withdrawn your support or love from someone because you couldn't "call the shots"? Actions like these are similar to jumping off the temple roof. Why? Because in each case you would have destroyed something by giving in to the temptation of the moment rather than standing firm in your knowledge that with God there is always a way.

How can you be sure that you are acting in God's way and not that of the sense consciousness? *You can tell by looking at the way you are handling the situation.* Are you standing on the roof about to jump, or are you sitting in the temple waiting for that still, small voice? Do you feel that there is no answer, no way out? Or do you know that even though the answer might not be readily apparent, it is there waiting for you to discover it? The sense consciousness would have you jump off the temple roof, destroying the possibility of harmony and healing. On the other hand, God's way is the way of life, not of destruction. With God, there is always an answer, always a solution, always a path of fulfillment. So why jump off the temple roof when you can take the stairs safely to the ground?

Choose the Kingdom You Shall Rule

Finally, the sense consciousness tried to convince Jesus that, as the Son of God, He deserved much more than He had already been given. As the scripture tells us, "Again, the devil (sense consciousness) took Him to a very high mountain, and showed Him all the kingdoms of the world and the glory of them." And the sense consciousness said to Jesus, "All these I will give you, if you will fall down and worship me." Jesus' answer was firm and to the point: "Begone, Satan! for it is written, 'You shall worship the Lord your God and Him only shall you serve' " (Matthew 4:8-10).

The kingdoms of the world offered to Jesus were the false lures of prestige and riches. Certainly we all should strive to live in such a way that we become an influence for good and justice. Also, in an abundant universe, there is no need for any of God's children to live in a state of lack and limitation. There is nothing wrong in accepting the good God has in store for us or in seeking to ensure that good for others.

What the sense consciousness was offering Jesus, though, was something entirely different. In this case, nothing was important but the gratification of the senses and the exercising of power over others. In other words, the sense consciousness was trying to convince Jesus that the only kingdoms worth ruling are those outer kingdoms that others can see and be impressed by.

In reality, though, ruling the inner kingdom, the realm of your thoughts, is more important and more in line with what God would have us do. Did you know that your mastery of your inner kingdom is what determines what your experience in the outer kingdom of the world will be like? It's true. If you are the master of your thoughts, no other circumstance can have an adverse effect on you. You might find yourself facing difficult times. But if your thoughts about the situation are in order and peaceful, if you try to find the good in the situation rather than giving in to the seeming bad of it, then you will be in control of you. So resist that final temptation to bow down and worship your sense consciousness.

Control Your Thoughts or They Will Control You

Throughout my life, I have prayed, I have fasted, I have studied God's word. As a result, I have accepted the truth that *there is nothing in the universe but God.* I don't believe that there is an evil force in the universe, but I do understand that because we have created power, we can manufacture in thought anything we want. And if our thoughts continue to be uncontrolled, we can end up manufacturing something that we don't want!

The Revealing Word, a religious dictionary, tells us that "In individual consciousness the wilderness is symbolical of the multitude of undisciplined and uncultivated thoughts." We all have thoughts that are undisciplined (those thoughts that we allow to run wild) and uncultivated (those thoughts that we neglect and fail to steer into productive channels). Thus as we read of Jesus' temptation in the wilderness, we begin to understand the way in which each of us is tempted by the thoughts in our own private wilderness. When these thoughts remain undisciplined and uncultivated, they become our enemies because they lead us away from the realization of our highest good.

How to Handle the Wilderness

From the experience Jesus had in the wilderness, you and I can learn how to handle thoughts that shake our faith or lead us to do things that are not for our highest good. And make no mistake, *we will have such thoughts!* If Jesus Himself was tempted so strongly by His sense consciousness just after being baptized and anointed as the Son of God, imagine the extent to which we are likely to be tested! From the moment we wake up in the morning until we fall asleep again at night, we are constantly bombarded with thoughts that can slow us down or sidetrack us. It is how we handle these thoughts that determines who is in control of us.

Think about how many thoughts and images hit you from the outer world. Think about some of the things you see when you drive through the streets, some of the things you are apt to encounter on billboards. On each one there is a thought belonging to someone else. But the billboard makes the thought so attractive that you adopt it as your own. Things that you never consciously thought about needing are made to look so good on those billboards that you feel you just *have* to have them, even though at the heart level you know you can live very well without them. So what once was an *outer* thought is now an *inner* thought for you. It has become embedded in your subconsciousness.

The marketing department of a business thinks carefully about how to get an idea across to you, the consumer. Once you are exposed to the marketing idea—whether you see it on a billboard or on television or hear about it on the radio—once you get the idea, you take it into your subconscious. After it knocks around in your subconscious long enough, it begins to influence your conscious mind. Then one day you find yourself saying, "Umm. That just might be something I want to try!" Then what happens? The conscious and the subconscious minds come together to find a way to get the thing that started off as *somebody else's idea for you.* If it wasn't something that you really wanted, then you have been controlled by someone else.

What I am suggesting is that **we need to be consciously**

aware of what we allow to enter into our subconscious.
We do this by setting our thoughts on things above, on God.
God is expressed as love and strength and all good. If you choose
not to think about such things, you are more than likely going
to find yourself having negative experiences and ending up with
people, circumstances, and possessions that you don't really
want. Why? Because **we draw to us that which we think
about.**

Teacher Learns a Lesson

How does this work? Let's take a fairly common occurrence, the state of having negative feelings for a coworker. A
teacher once told me, for instance, that she and all of her fellow
teachers had great difficulty working for the principal who had
been assigned to their school that year. Every time this particular
teacher was around the principal, something in her just balled
up. She would feel a kind of gripping in her stomach. At faculty
meetings, she would disagree with every suggestion the principal
made. Sometimes there was nothing wrong with the suggestion,
but she had built up all these feelings that kept her from being
reasonable about the man's presence. Finally, the situation became so intolerable that she decided she had better look for
another job. She didn't want to leave, though, because she had
been at the school many years and truly loved her students and
had taught many children in the same families. At this point she
came to me.

First, I encouraged her to look at how the situation had
developed and to realize what was happening. An outer
thought—in this case, the thought that the principal was impossible to work for—had taken root in her subconscious.
Having accepted this thought as true, she began feeling it and
acting on it. She had made a conscious choice to resent the

principal. As I told her, there can be no resentment unless you first think it. Thinking resentment brought resentment into reality in her case. The lesson to be learned here is that if we can do that with negative thoughts—bring them into our conscious reality—we can do the same thing with positive thoughts.

Be Transformed by the Renewal of Your Mind

Paul tells us, "Be not conformed to this world, but be transformed by the renewal of your mind, that you may prove what is the will of God, what is good and acceptable and perfect" (Romans 12:2). Obviously, resentment and other negative emotions are not the will of God. Neither are such feelings good and acceptable and perfect. Therefore, can any good come from holding on to thoughts that are contrary to the will of God?

Facing the Facts

Truth makes you face yourself. That's why Truth hurts sometimes and people back off from it. Often we are elated during our early experiences with Truth: "I got a new car!" "I bought my dream house!" We may have early tangible results that we call demonstrations. However, as we grow in our spiritual unfoldment we discover that it takes persistent believing and affirming positive thoughts to continue to experience good.

Think on These Things

It need not be such hard work, though, if we take Paul's advice in Philippians 4:8 ". . . whatsoever things are true, whatsoever things are honest, whatsoever things are just, whatsoever things are pure, whatsoever things are lovely, whatsoever things are of good report; if there be any virtue and if there be any praise, think on these things.'' We need to learn to balance our thoughts. In doing so we will balance our experiences. Instead of dwelling on conflict and problems all the time, we can take time to send someone flowers, to listen to a symphony, to read inspiring works.

Throughout the Scriptures are words of wisdom and inspiration that can transform your life for the better.

If you take this Scripture and work with it for a long time, your life *will* be transformed. I've tried it; I *know it works*. You cannot be unjust if you think on things that are just. You cannot be deceitful if you think on things that are true. And you cannot speak unjustly, dishonesty, deceitfully, or falsely if you think always of the just, the honorable, the true.

Have you ever known a person who talked about everything without ever saying anything worth hearing? Such a person is not thinking about things of good report but about all the negative aspects of life. The subconscious picks up these negative thoughts and turns them into negative spoken words. Eventually such a person's affairs get messed up, and the person complains all the time, and begins to dislike people and to think that people don't like him or her. All this comes about because the person has allowed his or her conscious thoughts to run rampant with all the negative impressions of the world.

Admittedly it is not easy to always think good thoughts, because of all the negative images in the outer world. The key, however, is to *consciously be aware of where your thoughts are*. **When you consciously lift your thoughts upward, Godward, your experience can't help but follow.**

I Made Me Do It!

Have you ever seen a cartoon showing a person in struggle with himself? There sits a person in the midst of temptation. On one side is a little devil with horns and a tail. On the other side sits a little angel with halo and wings. The devil says one thing and the angel says something else. "Lie, steal, cheat!" the devil says. "You don't have to do any of these things," the angel says. What will the person do? Who will he or she give in to?

We all have conflicts of this kind and many times we make the wrong choice. In the 1970's, comedian Flip Wilson popularized the saying, "The devil made me do it." It was often used to deny responsibility for wrong choices. Now that we know that the devil is our sense consciousness, we can understand that what we are *really* saying is that putting our worldly self before our spiritual self is what leads to actions and choices we later regret.

Who's in Charge Here?

Who is in control of you? Who is it that "makes" you do things? By now you should understand that *it is some aspect of you yourself—not some outside force, some devil—that makes you do whatever you do.* When you allow your thoughts to run rampant, then your life experiences will reflect your inability to discipline your thoughts. When your mind keeps getting confused, who has the power to straighten it out? *You do!* What this means is that we have to stop blaming others for our undesirable experiences. **Only after we stop blaming others can we begin to take charge of our lives and turn things around to our satisfaction.**

One of the main reasons we fail to take charge of our lives is that a negative self-image keeps us from doing so. Jesus knew

His divinity, but we are still struggling to discover and believe in ours. The Scriptures tell us, "And the Word became flesh and dwelt among us, full of grace and truth; we have beheld His glory, glory as of the only Son from the Father" (John 1:14). Jesus, then, is the perfect idea of what God has in store for man; He represents God's idea of man in expression. That is why Jesus went through all the physical things we go through. He needed food; He needed air; He needed a place to sleep. He believed in self-preservation; He believed in self-actualization; He believed in self-esteem. He cried; He laughed; He joked. Yet for all His humanness, there was still that divinity.

So the spiritual being dwells in us all the time. Our challenge lies in integrating the spiritual and human natures of ourselves. We are now realizing that *we can humanly make a choice to accept the things of Spirit.* This is when the integration takes place. The mind no longer seeks to pursue just anything, to be in the world and have worldly pursuits. Once we reach this point, we no longer want to go back to old ways of thinking and being. And once we reach this point, our self-image develops by leaps and bounds, because we realize that we have the power and the will to choose for ourselves that which will bring to us our highest good rather than that which will tear us down.

Christ in You: The Hope of Glory

Realize, as Jesus taught, that you are the son or daughter of God. Don't let anybody fool you into thinking otherwise. You are not a worm of the dust, although you might have been conditioned to believe that. Let go of the feeling that you are "nobody." Tearing down does not build up. Whenever anyone approached Jesus, He never inquired about their background. He saw their Christ nature, their spiritual nature, their divinity. He went straight to that inner part of them even they didn't know was there. We need to get in the habit of going to that part within ourselves, and then we need to learn to go to that part within others.

The key to finding this divinity of our natures is to keep our thoughts on those lovely, pure, honest things of good report of which Paul spoke. All these things are of God. Think of your thoughts as traffic and yourself as the air traffic controller or police officer on the corner. You can direct your thoughts to the channels in which you want them to travel. And where your thoughts go, so goes your life.

Again, I ask, "Who is in control of you?" Are you comfortable living with the idea that some force you cannot control takes charge of you and makes you do things that end up making you unhappy and robbing you of your good? I find that a very unpleasant idea, and so I choose to believe that **I am in control of me,** and that with the help of God, I can make right choices that lead to happiness and fulfillment.

To condition your mind to seek the Truth and to focus your thoughts on your highest good, learn to use affirmations daily.

CHAPTER TWO

*

Affirmations and How to Use Them

*A*n affirmation is a positive statement of truth. To affirm is to make firm in your mind. It is stating something to be true regardless of all evidence to the contrary. It is a type of mind activity used for building consciousness (awareness). It lifts you out of false thinking. An affirmation contains the elements of your belief, attitude, and motivation. An affirmation is made up of words. Words charged with power, conviction, and faith will produce after their kind. Every time you speak, the atoms in your body are affected, and the rate of their vibration is either raised or lowered.

God has given us the power of the word to use. We should be selective in the choice of words we use, for they will become our experience.

The purpose of an affirmation is to impress the subconscious mind, for what is impressed is expressed. This is done by repetition, feeling, and imaging. Repeat over and over as often as possible the affirmation with conviction and authority, believing every word you say, and see it taking shape and form.

Repeat it until it becomes a part of you. In conclusion always give thanks.

It is also a good idea to give thanks before using an affirmation to prepare your subconscious to accept the truth of the affirmation.

Many people think that affirmations cannot bring about changes because the act of affirming is so simple in comparison to the difficulty of the problem they face. If that is your feeling, it may be that you have given so much power to the problem that it now appears overwhelming and unconquerable. The first thing you must do, then, is to change the way you think about your problem.

Instead of focusing on the problem, focus on the Truths of God. State your desired outcome and then say, "Thank you, God, for answered prayer." Then every time you think about the situation, substitute confidence for the feat thought. Act as though what you desire already *is,* and so it shall be.

Prepare a Mental Field

Suppose you have been using an affirmation over and over and find that it is not "working." Perhaps your failure to bring about results comes from the fact that you have not done the necessary work to prepare a proper mental planting field for the affirmation. An affirmation, like any thought, is a seed that takes root and grows. However, it must have the proper firmament to grow into what you intend it to be, and it must be sown in the right way at the right time in order to flourish. This is something Jesus knew well, as we can tell from the Book of Matthew, in which He talks at length about the sowing and reaping of seeds.

There is, for instance, the parable of the sower. Some of

the sower's seeds fell on the path and were eaten by the birds. Others of his seeds fell on rocky ground, sprang up immediately, and were scorched by the sun. Still other seeds fell among the thorns and were choked. Finally, there were those seeds that fell on good soil and multiplied thirty, sixty, or a hundred times (Matthew 13:3–8).

Jesus gave the disciples an explanation of what this parable meant in terms of the word of the Kingdom of God (see Matthew 13:18–23). There is another way of looking at this parable as it applies to the use of affirmations.

Seeds on the Path

Let us say, for example, that you have written an affirmation that you intend to use a healing treatment. Suppose you have given yourself the treatment over and over but see no results. Did you, perhaps, sow the affirmation on the "path," *the edges of your consciousness,* rather than let it sink into the depths of your subconscious where it could take root? How can you tell if the affirmation is falling on the path and not in the depths of your subconscious where you intended it to be? Well, you might find yourself thinking of other, unrelated matters while you are giving the healing treatment. In that case, the affirmation has been crowded out, so to speak, pushed to the edges of your consciousness while the other matters occupied the area of your mind where the real work is done.

Seeds on Rocky Ground

What about the affirmation that falls on rocky ground? Your rocky mental ground might consist of *worry, fear, or doubt about the outcome* of what you are treating. If this is your state of mind, you are like the disciples, despairing because while crossing the sea—*with Jesus right there in the boat with them!*—they had only one loaf of bread (Mark 8:13–16). Can you imagine being in a boat with Jesus and worrying because you have only one loaf of bread? If that is your state of mind, you haven't yet accepted the power of Jesus to heal every condition, to fill every need, to comfort every sorrow. "Why do you discuss the fact that you have no bread?" Jesus asked the disciples on this occasion. "Do you not yet perceive or understand? Are your hearts hardened?" (Mark 8:17).

Seeds Among Thorns

There are also affirmations that seem to take root but are smothered by thorns—*negative thoughts*. These thorns didn't "just come from nowhere." No, they were there all along. Mental thorns are feelings of resentment, bitterness, jealousy, malice, hatred—all the twisted, loveless feelings that eat at one's insides and destroy the person who holds them. An affirmation, on the other hand, by its very nature says, *I want my highest good and that of everyone I encounter.* You can't make such a statement and mean it while you are a breeding ground for mental thorns.

Seeds on Good Soil

In other words, it is only those affirmations that fall on good soil which will manifest in your life *and* have lasting results. An affirmation sown on rocky ground might sprout a little, like the sower's seed that sprang up very quickly after falling on rocky ground. You might see some quick changes in your life, but they may not last because they were not planted in the soil of deep faith and thanksgiving. You might experience these same quick and short-lived results from affirmations sown on the path of your consciousness or in the midst of thorns. The parable, after all, did not say that the seeds sown in the unfavorable places did not grow at all. No, except for the seeds the birds ate all the others grew. This is why people who don't seem to "deserve" something good often get it. But don't be deceived by appearances, now that you know what happens to seeds improperly sown.

Only *you* know what kind of mental gardening you must do before you sow your affirmations. Only *you* know where you are in consciousness. But wherever you are when a message is given, a healing treatment is expressed, a song is sung, or an affirmation is offered, there will be that in you which will reach you at your level of awareness. Wherever you are, give thanks and go from there. You don't have to be like your neighbor. You only have to be aware of where you are, of how much you are seeking to further understand yourself and what you are. Once you achieve this awareness and work with it, the achievement of your affirmation is on the way.

AFFIRMATIONS

1. *God is the potential that expresses through me.*
2. *Today is my day to put aside all that worried me yesterday.*
3. *I express love on every level, with God, myself, and my fellow human beings.*
4. *I am in divine order in my thinking and in my relationships.*
5. *The love of Jesus Christ within me gives me the ability to forgive fully and freely.*
6. *I am divinely protected at all times, in all places, and under all circumstances.*
7. *Prosperity is my divine birthright.*
8. *I deserve the best as a Child of God.*
9. *I have faith in God in me to heal my condition.*
10. *I am a unique, unrepeatable miracle!*
11. *I do not look to things, outer conditions, and people to bring me peace and happiness.*
12. *I open my consciousness of love for my business, producing overflowing profits.*

*

CHAPTER THREE

Turn Your Fear into Faith

*W*e all want the most out of life, but few of us know how to get it. One thing we do realize, however, is that to get the most out of life, we must be willing to make some changes. Yet so many of us are afraid of the outcome. Change, after all, means replacing one thing with another. Suppose we fail in our efforts. Then we would have discarded our old familiar way of doing things for a new way that didn't work. Or suppose we succeed in our efforts, only to find that we don't like what the change demands of us. Suppose the change seems to cut out some of our fun or causes us to do without something we truly enjoyed. Then what?

Fear of an undesirable outcome or fear of failure can immobilize us to the point that we lose all opportunity to grow and to experience the fullness of life. However, what we need to understand is that if we have received from God the idea that we need to make changes in our lives, then we need only apply our faith to that idea and be patient in the working out of the change. The following four steps will help you move fearlessly through changes with complete faith that the outcome will be for your highest good. These steps are **(1): work at being a balanced person; (2) expect every day to be your fullest day; (3) make decisions and stick to them;** and **(4) take action.** If you undertake each step in faith rather than fear, not only will you achieve what you want, but you will be happy with what you achieve. Let's look more closely at each of these four steps.

1. Work at Being a Balanced Person

From time to time we all face situations that we'd rather not have to deal with. Perhaps a difficult meeting awaits us at work, or there might be a painful conflict at home that simply must be worked out. Or the challenge may be something internal, such as a difficult decision or trying to overcome fear, doubt, illness, or a damaging habit. Whatever the situation, our human resources alone may not be sufficient for handling the imbalance.

At such times, what a blessing it is to know that we are endowed with certain faculties of mind that we can use to keep ourselves in tune, in contact with the Christ consciousness. We can be renewed and transformed in mind and in body, for instance, when we call forth the faculty of strength.

When we talk about the faculty of strength, most people think of power, of being a great might. But strength is also expressed on the spiritual level, and it must first be in that respect that you understand strength. There is no power, there is no might, there can be no physical expressions unless one understands the inner foundations of strength. You already have built right into your soul the strength that you need. As within, so without. Therefore, what you have to do is draw from the inner in order to produce the kind of outer experience that you want to bring yourself into balance.

There are certain easy-to-learn steps that will help you master the technique of turning within for strength. The first thing you'll have to do is regain control of your thoughts and reactions to the threatening situation. Have you ever heard someone say, "I feel like I just want to cry. If I could, I know I'd feel so much better." Well, if you ever feel that way, then go ahead and have a good cry. Often, day-to-day tension and frustrations cause us to react on an emotional level. When you get into that level of consciousness where crying seems like the only release, then it just may be the best thing for you. Crying, you see, is a form of releasing anxiety; and when you are crying, you begin to leave behind the tension and the feelings of defeat and depression. Not until you accomplish this can you begin to feed your conscious mind with thoughts of strength.

When you release tension and feelings of defeat, there is that in you which begins to pick up; and somehow you just know that it's going to be all right. Philippians 4:13 tells us that *"I can do all things through Christ which strengthens me."* So just by speaking and truly believing words of Truth, you begin to have the lifting up from that level of not knowing which way you're going. But in order to do this, you have to still yourself. The key to all this is, *"Be still and know that I am God"* (Psalm 46: 10). Become still so that you can feel and know that inner strength, that strength of God which surpasses all understanding.

I often say to the men in our church, "If you feel like crying, CRY!" That's a belief system our culture has promoted: "Men don't cry." How often do we need to be reminded that Jesus set the example for men expressing their emotions? We find this example in the Book of John when Jesus was going to the bedside of his sick friend, Lazarus. By the time He arrived, He found the villagers trying to comfort Lazarus' sisters, Mary and Martha. Seeing Jesus, Mary went to Him and fell at His feet, crying, "Lord, if you had been here, my brother would not have died." The Scripture goes on to say that "When Jesus saw her weeping, and the Jews who came with her also weeping, He was deeply moved in spirit and troubled; and He said, 'Where have you laid him?' They said to Him, 'Lord, come and see.' Jesus wept" (John 11:32–35).

So all you men reading these words, please know that whenever you can let go and release that pressure—in your wife's arms, your girlfriend's arms, with a friend, or alone—it doesn't matter where, *just do it*. If you need to let go, don't keep it within, because holding pressures within is the beginning of stress. Some of us pay hundreds of dollars for stress control. Thank God the ideas have come to help us when we have gone too far. But if we knew how to be balanced people, we could save ourselves much money.

Recognize Your Multidimensionality

Being balanced means first recognizing that *there is more than one dimension to us* and then allowing that other, unrecognized dimension to find expression. In recent years, for instance, there's been a lot of talk about the "left brain" and the "right brain." The theory is that all people are dominated by one side of the brain or the other. If the left brain dominates, a person tends toward intellectualism; if the right brain dominates, creativity is the predominant characteristic. Both intellectualism and creativity have their place, though, and so somehow we've got to achieve a balance between the two.

The physical being also has more than one dimension. Our natural inclination is toward health, although sometimes disease and pain will intrude upon that health as a means of warning us that something is wrong somewhere. Perhaps you haven't had a vacation in a long time and your body is feeling the stress. This is such a well-known fact that you often see in newspapers or magazines a "stress chart" showing different stressful factors that can accumulate and lead to predictable illness.

Disease and pain, in other words, can play an important role in our lives. But we don't want to be dominated by disease or pain, or we would live very uncomfortable, unproductive lives, because we would be spending all our time fighting off ailments of one kind or another. Therefore it is important to learn how to establish and maintain balance.

Balance Through Imagination

Realize that you have the power to achieve this balance. One way to do so is to **draw on your power of imagination.** If I describe something that I witnessed, something that you were not there to witness, you are able to "see" what I'm talking about by using your "third eye." You can use that part of your brain containing nerves that help you form a picture. This "third eye" can be used to develop either the intellectual or the creative aspect of a person's character. It can also be used to bring about improvements in physical conditions, your social life, or nearly anything you can think of.

As you use your power of imagination, use it to form pictures of goodness. We seem to have no trouble forming pictures of things that are terrible. You can reverse this tendency, though, and begin forming pictures of beautiful things. Go to bed at night with something beautiful on your mind. Play some good music or read a good book. Read something inspirational. **Begin to train your own brain to think positively.**

These good thoughts that you can teach yourself to think apply to every aspect of your life. We know in truth that we have not used the fullest capacity of our brain cells. We also know that the cells of our body are intelligent. We know that, and yet we do nothing about it. You can talk to your body, though, and it will respond. You can say, *Body, let me just love you a little bit.* Yes, you can!

I once talked to a young woman who told me she had arthritis. I said, "Just massage your knee once in a while. Just love that knee and bless that knee. Watch the power you have to bring the healing."

Sometimes the healing doesn't come quickly because we have thought negatively for so long, and so many of our conversations are negative. **We need to raise our consciousness to realize that things are still beautiful, still encouraging, still possible.** The problem is that with so much negative chatter, we often don't see the beauty, encouragement, and possibility in things. At such times, we can turn the situation around by the use of positive affirmations.

Visualize the Good

Once when addressing a group of businesspeople, I told about a habit I developed when my church moved into the building it occupies. There were forty people sitting in an auditorium that seated some 250. We would go there on Sunday and there seemed to be miles and miles of empty pews. There was a little box-like area where I would go and stand before services. I would look out at the congregation and say, *Thank you, Father, for the people that are coming.* I was visualizing, using my imagination. Then I would go to the church on Saturdays and walk down every aisle and row, saying, *Thank you, God! Thank you for people!*

Some acquaintances who knew I did this thought I was crazy. You too, as you read this, may think that I was crazy.

However, let me tell you one thing: it worked. So if you have a business that isn't flourishing, begin visualizing people coming into that place of business. Use your power of imagination. Get up every day and say, *Thank you, Father, for my business. Thank you for my customers.*

Some of you business owners may be thinking as you read this, "Well, business *could* be better, but it's the off-season." My answer to that is, there are no off-seasons of Infinite Intelligence. I've seen people sell real estate at the slowest "season." I've seen businesses flourish at the seasons when they were not supposed to, because the proprietors believed they were not just sitting in that business. Instead, they believed that they were there to give something back to the world through whatever it was that they were selling or producing.

That's the power of imagination that we all have. That's the power of faith that you must use in order to believe that you aren't in business without cause. It's the same faith that enables you to say, when you send your children off to school, *Thanks, God. Take care of them all day.* Then you can go on to work and not be anxious or worried. Visualize balance in your life and be prepared to see change happen.

2. Expect Every Day to Be Your Fullest Day

When the congregation at Hillside where I preach leaves the service on Sundays, I often say, "Members and friends, this is the start of the greatest week you have ever had." You know, when you start affirming something like this, **you begin to look for something good to happen to you.** Living with that expectation will replace the negative programming to which we are subjected.

We're Programmed—But for What?

We are all extremely programmed by what we are exposed to. Take, for instance, a message we frequently hear on television: "Take Sominex and sleep tonight." You hear that often enough and your subconscious mind becomes programmed. Oh, you may not react right away. But one day you walk into a drugstore and out of nowhere you remember that you haven't been sleeping well. You rush to the counter and say, "Where's the Sominex, where's the Sominex?" Programmed.

There are times when I reach the point where I am so negatively programmed that I don't even pick up a newspaper. There are certain times when I can't take the news because it all seems so devastating. I'm being programmed to believe that every day is my last day. Now I want to be programmed to **believe that every day is my *fullest* day.**

As I say, we are all programmed. But if we can be programmed negatively, we can also program ourselves positively. If, for instance, you would program yourself to believe in yourself and in what you are doing, you would do yourself a world of good. You see, your mind is like a garden. Every seed you put there will grow and develop the way you nourish it. If weeds grow up, it is because you've allowed the negative stuff to grow there.

The mind is like a computer disk: You can erase what someone else has stored on the disk and store whatever *you* want on it. And **if you accidentally begin to put something negative on your disk, just say, "Cancel, cancel."** Some computer systems even allow you to enter this very command on the keyboard. When I first learned the power of "Cancel, cancel," I thought it was a wonderful concept, and I found that it works beautifully to keep the negative thoughts from finding a place in the tapes of my subconscious.

Your Word Has Power

Perhaps you haven't yet realized the power of the word. Once it goes out, it takes on flesh. That is why when we try to recall experiences, we don't remember what we have said. Day to day, our experiences come and go, and afterwards we often cannot see our life in its entirety. However, we can begin to reconstruct our daily experience by applying the law of cause and effect. When we see the effect, we should begin looking for the cause. *Often we will find that the cause had its origin in the words we thought or said.*

If we are always expecting *this day* to be our fullest, however, chances are we will get in the habit of using the words we speak and the words we think to help make it so. Knowing that the word has power to bring about unpleasant consequences, we can turn it to our advantage and use it to bring about the consequences we want. If we expect each day to be our fullest, we will not likely set in motion anything that will keep it from being so.

Expect More Good

In addition to speaking words to shape our good, we also can use good experiences to teach us how to expect *more* good experiences. One of my favorite childhood memories, for instance, is eating Cracker Jacks. Didn t you eat them too? Why did you eat them? What made you like them so much? Tell the truth. Did it have something to do with the prize at the bottom of the box? After your first box of Cracker Jacks, or after you had just watched your friend eat the first box of Cracker Jacks you ever saw, you were programmed to expect a pleasant surprise at the bottom of every box of Cracker Jacks.

In the same way, we can let our good experiences teach us

to expect more of the same. Why should good be a onetime experience? Why shouldn't we expect to repeat the successes of our lives, to relive happy moments, to reexperience joy and beauty? **Let one good experience teach another how to happen.** And let your good experiences program you to be receptive to "repeat performances."

3. Make Decisions and Stick to Them

Some people are chronic worriers. They love to worry. Have you ever met people like that? They have to tell you about their worries, simply because they have not learned that the energy they spend with worries could be used to sit down and make plans. Instead of worrying, they could look at the situation and decide that it does not have power over them.

Decide is the key word. Consider the case of the man who lay by the pool for thirty-eight years (John 5:2–11). An angel would come and trouble the waters at regular intervals. If one could get into the pool at that particular moment, healing would take place. But every time the angel came (and I take it from the Scriptures that it was not an everyday occurrence), this sick man would wait for someone to either pick him up and place him in the pool or help him get to it so that he could lower himself into the waters.

Someone said he could have just rolled over into the water. Yes, he could have. But for thirty-eight years, he just lay there until Jesus asked him if he wanted to be healed. Without laying a hand on him, without moving him any closer to the water than he had ever been, Jesus told the man to take up his pallet and walk. And he did. What was it that was touched? Certainly not the man's body. It must have been his mind. He must have *decided*. He made up his mind that he not only *could* be healed but *would* be as soon as he followed the order Jesus gave him.

Are You "Lying by the Pool"?

Some of us are just like that man by the pool. We are just "out there by the pool." We won't make a decision, won't move with an idea. Jesus said, "Get up!" And the man heard Him. His mind suddenly turned to the Truth. It's almost as though he said, "You mean I can get up? After all these years?"

In the same way, some of us must **learn to make decisions** about our lives. We don't have to stay in a rut. We don't have to accept classifications that others place on us. We don't have to be limited by experience or appearance.

For instance, I grew up in Houston, Texas, on Saulnier Street. When it rained on Saulnier Street, there was nothing but mud. My grandmother would go out in the back and get some wooden planks, which she kept there for that purpose, and lay them across the yard. I would step on the planks until I reached a good, solid place in the road that wasn't washed away by rain, then I went on to school.

My grandmother also cooked good meals every day. We went to her garden and picked fresh vegetables, yet I didn't know that because I didn't have meat every day I was eating in some kind of unusual way.

Many years later, as a student at Atlanta University, I learned that I had been raised in a ghetto. "What ghetto?" I demanded to know. "We just ate a lot of vegetables and our street got muddy when it rained, that's all!"

Now, many years after I was "enlightened" about my misfortune of being raised in a ghetto, the Western world has discovered that we do our bodies a disservice by eating meat every day! We have prescribed words and meanings for everything—

classifications, labels. Too bad these classifications sometimes have the effect of making us move away from what the tenderness of life is all about.

4. *Take Action*

When I walked out of Atlanta University with a Master's degree in Social Work, I thought I was the best social worker in the world until I got to Chicago and became involved on a practical rather than a theoretical level. Once I saw what being a social worker was all about, there were times when nothing that the professors had taught me worked. That's not to say that what I had learned was not good. But there were times when I sat in my office and said, *What do I do now? How do I handle teenage girls coming back from the summer break pregnant? How do I work with senior citizens whose only mail is an announcement from an agency or an advertisement? What do I do?*

There was nothing in the books to help that kind of reality. Sometimes I would sit for hours, days, or minutes. All of a sudden a little thought would come to me that was in no one's book, and I would have the courage to act on that flow of thought. This way of handling my job eventually earned me a reputation as one of the best social workers in Chicago, not because of anything *Barbara* did or had done, but because that Intelligence, that Essence, that Spirit, that Presence within me *and within you* went to work for me.

I know for a truth that there aren't any of you reading this book who have not had ideas seemingly from out of nowhere. You probably dismissed most of those ideas because you weren't sure about them. But I'm here to tell you, **make a decision now not to be afraid when these hunches come.** Realize that they are coming from a deeper source than you would ever dream. Use them! Take action! They work.

The Many Faces of ACTION

Taking action doesn't always mean something dramatic. There are many ways in which you can take action. Reading something inspirational is taking action, for while reading, you are absorbing positive thoughts that will motivate you to take the next step. Giving thanks is taking action, for it moves you to a consciousness of good in your life, and that consciousness paves the way for more good as discussed previously under "Expect Every Day to Be Your Fullest Day." In other words, **don't overlook the value of any action, no matter how small it may seem.**

Another important point about taking action is that it must be done regularly. Don't take for granted that anything will always be as it is, simply because it is so at a given moment. You may be a highly successful person. You may have everything you need in the way of material possessions—a beautiful home, luxury items, whatever. However, you also may have discovered that it's possible to be successful materially and still feel like a failure inside. This is because you may not have an appreciation of yourself as a person, as a human being, as a spiritual being, as a person who came to give something. It is a truism that many people have money and still are not happy. Many people have money and do not have what they value most, their health.

At a meeting I attended in Las Vegas with the International New Thought Alliance, Norman Cousins was honored as the Humanitarian of the Year. This is a man who took action when he was told he had a terminal illness. He would not accept the diagnosis. Instead he took action on his own and defeated the disease.

Let me make clear that I bless all doctors because doctors are instruments of God. However, as most doctors themselves will tell you, doctors cannot heal you. The doctor can prescribe and work with you, but *you* are the one who has to have a healing consciousness. I speak from experience. Having been a tubercular patient, I know what it means to lie flat on my back in a sanitarium for four years. I know what it means to have a healing because I kept repeating this prayer:

God is my help in every need.
God does my every hunger feed.
God walks beside me, guides my way,
Through every moment of the day.

I now am wise, I now am true,
Patient, kind, and loving, too.
All things I am, can do and be
Through Christ the Truth that is in me.

God is my health, I can't be sick.
God is my strength, unfailing quick.
God is my all; I know no fear
Since Light and Love and Truth are here.

This poem, called the "Prayer of Faith," was written by Hannah Korhaus. It says everything we need to know about the nature of God in us expressing as health and well-being. It brought me through many a dark moment, and it can do the same for you.

Claim Your Faith

My bout with tuberculosis occurred when I was an undergraduate at Texas Southern University. When I went back to school, I found that all my classmates had graduated while I was in the hospital. I went back into a class with younger women, such as Congresswoman Barbara Jordan and others who came to Texas Southern at that time. Yet there I was, and working as a maid on the campus was my only way to get through school. Despite appearances, I somehow knew that if I took action, everything would be all right.

Several years later when I was on a ship, sailing from Helsinki, Finland, to Leningrad, Russia, it suddenly struck me out in the middle of the Baltic Sea, *My God, my goodness! Here I am, on my way to Russia!* Looking at my background, it didn't seem possible. Here I was, the child whose grandmother had to place planks over a muddy yard so she could get to the road to walk to school, the young woman who had spent four years in a tubercular sanitarium, the young woman who then worked her way through college as a maid—here I was, invited all the way to Finland to present a professional paper in Helsinki!

I never ever dreamed that there was enough faith in the world to make something like that happen. There is enough faith to believe anything, though, and it is this same faith that you must claim for yourself. Claim it! Young people, children, adults, retirees, those imprisoned by bars or beliefs—claim it for yourself now! Don't let anybody tell you that you can't be what you want to be. Claim it and be it! Claim it through faith right now. Believe in yourself. Believe that you have something to give to the universe!

That, in essence, is the secret of taking action as a means of overcoming fear. If you *claim* what you want and believe in your ability to accomplish it, then you have banished the demon of fear that would keep you from reaching out for what you desire. *If you begin to think of your desired goal as yours, then you realize there is nothing to fear.*

Putting It All Together

Now what would Jesus have to say about this four-step method of turning fear into faith? I think He would agree with it because all it really amounts to is the same message He gave us: "Ask and ye shall receive" (Matthew 7:11). In order to ask for something, you have to decide that it is something good for you, something that in some way will bring balance into your life. So right away there are two of the four steps—**(1) seek to be a balanced person** and **(2) make decisions about what you want in life.**

Once you have named the thing you want and then decided that it will contribute to your becoming a balanced person, you have transformed the desire. No more is it a fuzzy, fearful unknown. Now you begin to look at it as part of the abundance of God's universe and you know that when it becomes yours, you can handle it. Knowing you can handle it, you no longer fear it.

Something else you will find, once you have asked God for what you want, is that the pursuit of your goal will contribute toward making each day fuller. There is nothing like having a goal to make you look forward to each day with anticipation. For all you know, today could be the day that you achieve your goal or at least make a major step in the completion of it. With that kind of incentive, you can't help but think positive thoughts, you can't help but believe in yourself and in your ability to do and be what you want.

With such an attitude, everything you do will be done in a spirit of thanksgiving. If you have a job serving others, you will want to say, *Thank you, God, for giving me this opportunity to be of service to others as they work toward their own unfoldment.* If you are self-employed, you will want to say, *Thank you, God, for giving me the resources to work toward my goals in my own way and in my own time.* If your paycheck comes from another and you are trying to get to the point of independence, you will want to say, *Thank you, God, for this base of support while I work on my goals.* In other words, no matter what you are doing on the way to fulfilling your desires, you will understand the way in which everything else you do fits into the scheme of things. You will understand the way in which all things work together for good to those who love the Lord, as it says in Romans 8:28. Having this understanding and this attitude is what makes a *full* day of fulfillment and joy for you and for all with whom you come in contact.

Plans Lead to Decisions

Once you name what it is that you want and ask for it, you will find yourself making decisions almost effortlessly. The decisions you make will be the ones you need to make in order to arrive at your goal. Immediately you will begin to understand that you can't have a goal in mind and no plan in mind. I repeat: **You can't have a goal in mind with no plan in mind.** And what is a plan but a series of decisions? First I will do this, then I will do that, and so on. Those are decisions, and guess what a decision leads to?

Decisions Lead to Action

That's right, *action*—the fourth step. Now, knowing what you want, you are in a position to take directed action toward achieving your goal. If you had started with this step, taking action before you had done your spiritual homework (that is, prayer and faith-building and positive thinking), chances are your actions would have had few or disastrous results. That's why *action is always that last step.* **You must prepare for this**

step with prayer, meditation, and cleansing of the mind.
The action that you are led to take will then be informed action,
informed by the still, small voice within.

The Four Steps in Jesus' Healings

If you examine some of the healings that Jesus performed,
you will see that they followed this same pattern. (1) He first
got the person to see himself as a balanced person. "Do you
want to be healed?" He often asked. Putting this question to the
person forced the person to think of himself as a balanced person,
to consider the possibility that the disease was balanced by a
spiritual aspect that was disease-free. In other words, even when
we are feeling physically drained or mentally depressed, there is
that *other* dimension of us which balances and even outweighs
the weariness.

(2) Once Jesus led the person to the realization of balance,
the person was in an expectant mood. What did he expect? To
be healed and, therefore, to experience the fullest day of his life.
(3) At this point, it was time for a decision. Jesus obviously had
already made His decision. Jesus would help the person experience healing. But the person who needed the healing had to
decide to *accept* healing and, having made that decision, had to
stick to it.

(4) Finally, having brought the person to a realization of
himself as a balanced person who had made a decision to let *this*
day be the fullest of his life, Jesus was ready to take action and
to lead the person to action. Jesus' action varied from healing to
healing. Sometimes He merely spoke to the person—as with the
man lying by the pool. Sometimes He spoke to the negative
forces within the person—as in the case of the epileptic child
(Mark 9:14–28). Sometimes He would touch the person—as
when He touched the eyes of the blind man (Mark 8:22–25).

Other times He would simply acknowledge the action others had taken on their own behalf—as when the woman with a hemorrhage touched the hem of His garment (Matthew 9:20–22).

In any case, Jesus always took action after the way had been prepared. And after the person He was healing took action on his or her own. The action might have been to stand up and walk, to open the eyes and see, to rise from the dead. It varied according to the need of the individual.

In the same way, the action that you are finally led to take—after taking the three preparatory steps—will lead to the realization of your goal. It matters not whether that goal is healing, a new job, a new home, a new attitude. You will know what actions you need to take because you will know what action you *haven't* taken up to this time. That is usually the key. "I've tried *everything*," people often say. My advice is to **try God first** and save yourself some time and effort.

A Note to Uncertain Believers

Perhaps you are concerned at this point about the strength of your belief in God's power to effect change in your life. You may want to believe that all things are possible through prayer and the four steps to change, but believing in these things is not exactly a popular modern-day concept. Most often we choose to be questioning and doubtful instead, like Doubting Thomas, the disciple who believed in the Lord—up to a point (John 20:19–31).

How can you have both belief and disbelief? Consider this: Has someone ever asked you a question and you weren't quite sure of the answer but you knew *something* about the subject? If that has ever happened to you, you might have answered, "I think so." In other words, you had belief—*you believed you knew the answer*—but you also had unbelief—*you weren't sure that your answer was the right one*. So rather than saying you didn't know, you simply said, "I think so."

Here's another example: In the Book of Mark, we find the story of Jesus curing a young boy of an illness that so baffled the people of the time that the boy was thought to be possessed by a demon. One day the boy had a seizure in the presence of the disciples and a crowd of townspeople. Everyone was quite agitated by what they had just seen, and the disciples ran excitedly to Jesus. The boy's father followed them and told Jesus that he had brought his son to Him because of the demon that possessed him. While they talked, the boy had another seizure.

"If you can do anything, have pity on us and help us," the boy's father pleaded.

"If you can believe!" Jesus responded. "All things are possible to him who believes."

"I believe," said the boy's father; "help thou mine unbelief" (Mark 9:22–24).

Do you follow the man's reasoning? By this time, Jesus had quite a reputation. He had already fed thousands with a few loaves of bread and some small fish; He had restored speech and hearing to a deaf mute; He had restored sight to the blind. So the man was inclined to believe that Jesus had some kind of power that no one else possessed.

But *just in case* all these miracles and healings were somehow "different," the man decided to throw an "if" into his plea for help. That way, you see, he would not be "putting Jesus on the spot" as we might say. He would leave Him an "out." By approaching the matter in this way, the man was also leaving himself an out. He would not put all his hopes on this one chance. Thus, if Jesus couldn't cure the child, the father's disappointment wouldn't be as great as if he believed without doubt.

This is an intellectual analysis of why the man would say he believed in one breath and turn around in the next breath and say, "help thou mine unbelief." Knowing human nature, we can imagine that the man's thought process was probably pretty much as I have described it above. We all go through the same kind of arguing back and forth with ourselves—weighing all the possibilities, discarding one way of looking at things in favor of another way. After so much of this kind of mental activity, we are more confused than ever. In the end, we often act on impulse, going with the feeling that is strong enough to win out over all the others. When we act on that impulse after all the intellectual wrestling, we are attuning ourselves to that still, small voice within. This intuition is God speaking to us.

So we can conclude that the boy's father probably had weighed all the possibilities and had finally decided—with some lingering doubts—to "try Jesus." Let's not be too hard on him for having doubts, though. Instead, we should give him credit for knowing and having the courage to admit that his belief wasn't as strong as it could be. Sometimes we too simply need to say, "Lord, I believe; but there is still a part of me that just hasn't caught up. Help me." That cry for help *will* be heard and answered, as it was in the case of this man and his son, and you will start to achieve balance in your life.

Of course, Jesus helped the father and son. He ordered the "demon" out of the body and told it never to come again. After one final seizure, the "demon" fled from the boy. The boy was so still that the crowd said, "He is dead." But Jesus took the boy by the hand and lifted him. The demon was no more (Mark 9: 14–28).

So if you find you are not quite sure *what* you believe, or *if* you believe, or if you even believe *enough,* talk to the Lord about it. He knows how you feel, how you are longing to get your life on course. And He has brought you to this place, even got this book into your hands, so that you might begin the journey toward a more fulfilling life. And every journey begins with the first step, no matter how small.

Listen to the voice within. Start your journey. Just knowing you are taking action toward that one, small goal will make you start to feel better, and your strength will grow. Soon you will realize that as you have grown, your belief has grown as well.

AFFIRMATIONS

1. I am not anxious over anything, as I place God first in my life.
2. I stand firm and hold to the truth that God in the midst of me reveals all answers.
3. I place my trust in God.
4. God is my hiding place and I am safe and secure.
5. God will keep me from all trouble.
6. I will not be afraid, for wherever I am, God is.
7. I release all struggle and anxiety for I know God is with me always.
8. Nothing or no one can keep my good from me.
9. I am filled with the freedom of Spirit.
10. I am a victor and not a victim.

CHAPTER FOUR

* * *

The Power of Prayer

It seems as though we are becoming a nation, a people, of constant worry. When I think about worry, I am reminded that worry means a distressful state of mind. It means anxiety. It means sometimes getting caught up in an experience without seeing an answer for that particular experience.

Recently I was on a plane, flying to another city for a speaking engagement. A very prominent businessman sat next to me and we began a conversation. As soon as my seatmate learned that I was a minister, he began telling me about a personal situation that he was going through. In fact, he was on his way home to work out some challenge with his wife. He had been away, and this time of separation was to give them both an opportunity to come back together, to see if they could bring things to a wonderful unity.

Well, we talked for almost an hour. He was clearly seeking my advice, yet each time I responded to him, he'd say, "Yes, but. . . ." That was the tone of the entire conversation. I would suggest the power of prayer, suggest that he turn within and look at himself and then accept his wife as she was. He would respond by saying something like, "Yes, *but* I'm so worried. I really want to work it out, but I'm just worried about what is going to happen before I get home."

Every time I would say something to him that I felt would be helpful, it seemed to frustrate him even more. Eventually I realized that he didn't really want me to help him reach any answer.

Now that's one kind of worry—the kind expressed by people who always say, "Yes, but. . . ." Then there's another kind of worry—that which begins with, "What if?" What if I don't get the job? What if my health fails? What if I don't have enough money?

These are chronic attitudes on the part of many people. All of us have that tendency to want to worry about every little thing. We'd live far more effectively, however, if every time something unsettling happened in this human experience we'd go back to the words of Jesus—back, for instance, to the sixth chapter of Matthew, the thirty-third and thirty-fourth verses. I didn't realize, in fact, until I went back to that passage in preparing this message how much those two verses have meant to me in my life experience:

> But seek ye first the kingdom of God, and His righteousness; and all these things shall be added unto you.

> Take therefore no thought for the morrow; for the morrow shall take thought for the things of itself. Sufficient unto the day is the evil thereof.

However, when we allow ourselves to get into a state of confusion, to get into an attitude of constant worrying, we are really denying that there is a God of righteousness. We are not living every day to the fullest. We are simply saying that there is no answer to whatever the situation is about which we're concerned. But Jesus said, seek the kingdom first. Seek to go within. Seek God in everything. And then you won't have to be so concerned about tomorrow. In other words, **why worry about tomorrow when you can pray today?**

So now we've looked at some of the ways in which we worry—the "Yes, but . . ." and the "What if . . . ?" We've defined worry as simply being fearful, afraid that something is or is not going to happen. And we know that fear is the emotion that operates when we don't have faith. Faith in what? Faith in whom? Faith in a Presence, faith in an Intelligence that is the Creator of this universe. Prayer, then—the other side of the coin of worry—is a conscious act, not something you do haphazardly, but a conscious effort to commune with this Intelligence, this Infinite Spirit that we commonly call God.

We use the word *God* all the time. But we must recognize that God is a force that is everywhere. We have to remind ourselves over and over again that *God is,* that there is no place where God cannot be found, that God is all-powerful. God is love. God is intelligence. We use these and other attributes to define something that is so great and so wonderful and that operates in so many ways for our highest good that we cannot confine this wondrous Something to a simple definition.

Perhaps there is something you have been working on or desiring for a long time. Or perhaps there is a difficult decision you must make, or perhaps you are concerned for a loved one. It doesn't matter how small a thing may appear to be. It doesn't matter how big it may appear in your experience. **You simply have to know of a truth that** *God is all you need* **and that** *He is always everywhere evenly present.*

Take a moment and say, "God, this is (*state your name*); need I say more?" What you are saying is "There is nothing else to say!'' God loves you. God appreciates you. So there is nothing else to say but "Here I am. I don't really have to say anything else. I simply acknowledge that You and I are one." Even this simplest form of prayer can become your way of being in touch with the Lord.

All Things Work Together

A young lady in my church is a salesperson in the children's department of a prestigious department store. She earns minimum wage and depends on commissions to round out her income. One day she gave this testimony:

> Every day I get up and acknowledge my priorities by saying, "God, I am beginning my day with you. Send to me today the customers that I need to earn what I want to earn, to be what I want to be."
>
> One day, for some unknown reason, I didn't pray that prayer. I didn't even say anything like it, and I don't know why, because it has been my habit for so long. Around three that afternoon, I suddenly realized that we hadn't had a customer all day. All of us on the floor were talking about this strange situation. "What's happening? Nobody's buying children's things today."
>
> Suddenly it was like a lightbulb came on in my mind. I excused myself and went back to the stockroom. "Father," I said, "forgive me for forgetting that you are my priority. I didn't do my prayer work today. So right here and now I say, 'Father, I acknowledge that you are the Spirit; you are the attracting Power. Thank you for my customers.' "

This was around three. The store was to close at six. I walked out of the stockroom, and a lady walked up to me and said, "Will you wait on me, please?" She bought over $300 worth of merchandise. Before I could finish ringing up this sale, another lady walked up and said, "Will you wait on me?" This lady bought over $400 worth of clothes.

Before the store closed at six, the member had earned the amount she wanted to earn that day because between sales she remembered to go back into the stockroom and acknowledge that there was something great about her, in her, and all around her. Even if she hadn't gotten a customer that day, she would have gone back the next and gotten a zillion customers. Why? Because she would have held on to her belief in the working of the Law. The truth is that her faith set her free. She remembered her priority and changed a dismal situation into a joyous one.

God Is All There Is

How many times has something like this happened to you in other circumstances? Did you continue to let a bad situation get worse, or did you stop where you were and say, "Okay, there has to be an answer"? If you are an accountant who can't get her books to balance; if you are a door-to-door salesman collecting a lot of "no thank-you's"; if you are a bus driver being thrown off schedule because you keep getting stuck in one traffic jam after another—whatever the situation, the principle is the same: God is all there is; there is nothing else.

This is the basic Truth of the universe, so claim It, live with It. **Continue to be open to every Truth that you know.** To the ministry from the church's pulpit, to the ministry from the books you read, to the ministry from the inspirational tapes you listen to—be open. Continue to study if you really want to know the Truth, because the wisdom of God will feed your soul. You may open a particular book in the bookstore and glance through it and say, "Umm—this is a little deep for me." I can assure you of one thing: If you really desire to learn, to know, there is nothing too deep for God. The Spirit will reveal it to you, because Spirit is everywhere.

What Are You Holding Back?

Think about your own situation for a moment. What have you been holding back, what have you refused to use that has come through you with so much power, and sometimes with so much peace? And when you admit what you have refused to act upon, or to use, you must also realize how much fuller your life and your experiences would have been if you had simply acted on what Spirit gave you—whether it is an idea, a talent, or some particular service that you are destined to perform.

I have had several experiences where Spirit was telling me one thing though I was set on another. One such experience led me to the 1984 Democratic National Convention. I had not attended the state convention of the Georgia delegates. I had not been involved in the political arena. But at this particular juncture, my name was brought up because I was known to be very supportive of the National Rainbow Coalition, who were supporting their leader, Reverend Jesse Jackson, a candidate for the presidency of the United States.

On the day of the Georgia convention, I was in my office at the church. One of my staff said, "You're going to Macon to the convention, aren't you?"

I said, "No, I'm not going. I have some things I must do.

I am honored that my name is on the delegate list and that they want me to work with them, but today I just really have to concentrate on some things involving the church and the various ministries. Today God is my priority. And that's all there is to it. I'm not doing anything else today."

God *was* my priority, and I was acting that day on what I understood to be God's will. However, as it turned out, I was elected to the Democratic National Rules Committee, even though I wasn't at the Georgia meeting when the nomination was made. Several days passed before I learned of this. When I did learn of it, I realized that I had made one choice that day while God was making another. The choice I made had to do with my own unfoldment and with the unfoldment of the ideas that were being projected at my church, the Hillside Truth Center. But as I followed up on that choice, Spirit had gone ahead and done what needed to be done in another arena. Had I followed my sense consciousness, my human perception, I might have withdrawn my name from the committee. But it was clear to me that God had other plans.

It's Not Too Late

Fortunately, it is never "too late" to act on the prompting of Spirit. **Right now, today, you can make the decision to move out of the staleness into the stillness and say, "God this is** *(your name);* **need I say more?"**

I have a habit of carrying a little notepad to catch a flow of thought that is not prompted by my human efforts. You know how quickly ideas can come and then seemingly disappear into the universe if we don't capture them right away. They are like dreams in that way. Sometimes someone will be talking with me and I'll get an idea for a sermon or a program, and I'll stop right there and jot a note to myself. Sometimes several days or weeks may pass before I get back to the notes. But whatever I do, it is never too late, because the idea was one that God wanted me to have and to act on.

Recognizing, then, that God is everywhere, we must learn that prayer is simply turning to this Presence in whatever situation we find ourselves. We may not be able to see the Presence, but it becomes apparent whenever we still ourselves. This is what the psalmist meant when he wrote, *"Be still and know that I am God"* (Psalms 46:10). When you still yourself, your anxious thoughts will begin settling. You can put them aside by putting in their place the Truth during your time of prayer. You can find your balance.

Now I want to share with you some steps in prayer. Let me say first that to pray effectively, you must know that God is the only Presence, the only Power. When there seems to be something else operating in your life, remember that you are working the law of cause and effect as we discussed earlier. For every outer experience, there has to be a cause that comes from within you. So begin by recognizing that God is the only Presence, the only Power.

Step One: Purification and Relaxation

The first step in effective prayer is to dissolve the worry and purify your mind. That means, among other things, forgiving yourself for having allowed yourself to get entangled and upset because you couldn't face a particular situation for what it was. I don't care what a situation is, you have to face it before you can handle it. And worry simply says, "I don't want to face it."

I know it's easier to say, "I'm so worried . . . I don't see a way . . . I don't see the answer" than it is to face a given situation. If that is the way you initially approached your current challenge, then begin by forgiving yourself for having been at that level of consciousness. That's the purification—cleansing the mind, dissolving those mental blocks of anger, fear, doubt, excuses, self-pity, and blaming of others. Worry has all these things built into it, and you simply must cleanse your mind of them and forgive yourself and anyone else whom you might have held in thoughts of negativity.

Often, we try to call up our strength when we are upset or irritated about something. If that is the case, you might want to withdraw to a quiet place so that you can come down off that anger and irritability. Remember, we want to seek our strength in stillness. In your quiet location, sit in a relaxed way and feel yourself breathing the breath of God. Remember, breath is life, and life is God. If you've been under a lot of pressure, just feel yourself relaxing in body. Maybe you're having a challenge with a particular part of your body. Remember, you can speak the word of strength to that part of your body. Know that your words have the power to lift you up.

After you've relaxed your body, close your eyes for a moment and speak the Truth with this affirmation: *I still myself toward divine strength*. In this time of quiet, recognize that there is only one Power, one Presence, God the Good. That God is the strength of your being. If while doing this relaxation exercise you have the tendency to drop off and go to sleep, that's all right, because in that quietness and time of rest comes the strength to do what you have to do upon awakening.

Complete your relaxation exercise by declaring to yourself, *I feel myself full of divine strength*. The lifting in consciousness that you will feel at this point is also raising your body and your affairs to divine order.

Step Two: Illumination and Seeing Yourself in a Different Light

The word *light* appears many times in the Bible. What it expresses is the need to pray for the expansion and uplifting of your thoughts as you talk to God simply and naturally. Know too that you can talk to that Presence just as you would talk to a friend.

You see, when you forgive yourself for feeling foolish and out of place, for fearing that there was no answer, you then begin moving toward the point where you can say, *God, thank You for illumination. Thank You for light. Thank You for understanding and for showing me how to pray.*

This talking to God is so important. There are many times when I don't know what to say. There's just so much happening in the world that often I'll just get still and I'll say, *God, just feel my mind. Just help me to know how to lift my consciousness, to set my sights on things above. Help me, God, to transform my mind.* That's what Paul meant in Romans 12:2 when he said:

> And be not conformed to this world; but be ye trans-
> formed by the renewing of your mind, that ye may
> prove what is that good, and acceptable, and perfect
> will of God.

Most of us don't have very much patience with ourselves. That's why we are so likely to go out and buy the "extra-strength pain reliever" we see advertised. But once the physical pain has passed, the psychological or emotional pain remains.

The problem is still there, because we haven't learned to recognize that we have the power of that inner strength to see it through and to find an answer. But when you get in the habit of stilling yourself, you find that you have a great deal of patience.

You might also find that you are more tolerant of others than you thought you were. So often we are unfair to ourselves and to others because we can't tolerate people's differences. Sometimes we're not tolerant because someone doesn't belong to our religious denomination; because someone doesn't accept what we think is the greatest idea in the world; because someone has different values from the ones we hold. Whatever the differences, what we have to realize is that each person has the right to operate at his or her own level of awareness. So if tolerance is a stumbling block for you, try telling yourself, "Even though I disagree with this person, I can at least listen to what he's saying and be open to it and then proceed to work toward a solution in the way that's best for my experience." You never know how you might be blessed, what you might learn just from the simple act of listening with an open mind, knowing all the while that *you* can make up your own mind. You can still "see the light."

Step Three: Unification

So often when we are praying we don't fully recognize that during this time of prayer we can unify ourselves with God. We can become one with God, because the minute we still ourselves, the anxiousness has to move out of the way. It is at this moment in which the anxiousness falls away that we begin to feel no separation; then we know that God is right where we are. That Presence is ever available for us to unify ourselves with. That is what Jesus meant when He said, *"I and my Father are one"* (John 10:30). And this same Father is *your* Father.

Step Four: Petition

Ask God for your desire. You see, the desire is fulfilled through you, through the idea, through the attracting power of God that brings to you all that you need to achieve your goals.

Once you make your petition, once you state your request to the Father, you might, as many people do, experience some doubt whether you're praying for the "right" thing. Here, then, are some questions you can ask yourself to clear up this doubt:

First, *Is what I am praying for good for all concerned? Will having it hurt me or anyone else?*

Second, *Am I willing to give up something that I now have in order to make ready for my new good?* You see, whenever something good comes in, something else moves out. Are you willing for this to happen?

Third, *Am I willing to accept the responsibility for what I am asking?* With fulfilled desires goes the responsibility of making commitments, of making them work for you and following through on them.

If you can answer these questions to your satisfaction, then you can proceed with your prayers with a clean heart and a ready, receptive mind.

Step Five: Gratitude

Give thanks for what you have already received. In Matthew 6:32, Jesus tells us that our heavenly Father knows what we have need of even before we ask. What does this mean? It means that the good—whatever it may be—is already there for you. Accept it and give thanks for it.

You may have to begin today with just that act of forgiving

yourself for ever having worried in the first place. I've gone through many experiences in life, and I've seen God work. I've seen people without money, and I've seen God bring them what they needed despite their lack of money. For instance, have you ever been without money for food and someone invited you to dinner? That's God! I've seen so many channels open in this way that I *know* that if you will just get into a prayerful attitude and trust that Infinite Intelligence, that Infinite Spirit, God, to work out the perfect plan in your life, a way *will* open where there seemed to be no answer.

I want to suggest something to you that we've often done at Hillside. Take a box—maybe a shoe box, a tissue box, or a box that some small item you bought came in. Call this "God's Thank-You Box" and write on one side of it *Thank You, Father; Thank You, Father; Thank You, Father. And so it is.* You might also want to add some Scriptures, such as *"And all things, whatsoever ye shall ask in prayer, believing, ye shall receive"* (Matthew 21: 22), or *"My God shall supply all your needs according to His riches in glory by Christ Jesus"* (Philippians 4:19). Whatever Scripture you choose, it is simply to remind you that God is the answer, that God is always there. Not a man, not a figure, but a Presence, an ever-present help in time of trouble.

Finally, make a little slit in the top of the box and then put this box in its own special place. Every day, drop in your box a thank-you to God for something, if for no more than for your sense of smell, for your ability to talk. Find something every day for a week that you can thank God for, and place it in your Thank-You Box.

This box is simply a symbol of what God is in your life, an exercise to help you realize how much you are already receiving from the Father. As I say, we've done this at Hillside on occasion, and each time we do it, many people have shared with us afterwards how meaningful it was in reminding them that there are so many things in life, so much about us as children of God, that we can say thank you for.

So I say to you, **believe in the power of prayer.** Take the five steps suggested above and use your Thank-You Box if you need to. You'll find that those worries—whatever they are—can be turned around and transformed. If you are worried about money, say, *Thank You, Father, for the abundance that is mine.* If you are worried about your health, say, *Thank You, Father, for the wholeness that is mine.* If you are worried about how you are going to make it through the next day, say, *Thank You, God, for this day. This is the best day of my life.* And every time you say *Thank You,* write out what you're giving thanks for and drop it in your box.

Believe me, this conscious acting out of your prayers will make a difference, because it will serve to remind you to use your power of imagination to know that God is the answer to every situation, your refuge and your strength, a very present help in time of need. Through it all, *why worry when you can pray?*

AFFIRMATIONS

1. *The perfect Spirit is in control of my entire being, giving me perfect directions.*
2. *The love of God now controls my mind and all my affairs.*
3. *I give God thanks for all that I give and all that I receive.*
4. *I pray with unshakable faith in God, knowing with Him, all things are possible.*
5. *I pray with thankfulness, with joy knowing my God shall supply all my needs.*
6. *The presence of God indwells me and surrounds me.*
7. *I open my mind to the Spirit of Truth and I make right decisions.*
8. *The Spirit of wisdom is the only activity in my life now.*
9. *Spirit knows and always brings to my mind divine ideas.*
10. *I am never alone, God is with me always.*
11. *Peace, Peace, Peace, be still.*

CHAPTER FIVE

✳

Three Secrets to a Happy Life

$\mathcal{N}$o doubt you have seen bumper stickers and buttons which urge us to *Try Jesus!* When I see these words, I interpret them to mean that we should try His methods. My own experience was such that I did not come through Muhammad, the Buddha, nor some of the other teachers. But I have studied their works and I have discovered that every major religion in the world has the same threads of love, wisdom, and understanding. I have discerned that the Golden Rule is the same, no matter how it is worded. However, since Jesus Christ and His works are what I love, He is my major inspiration; and through Him, I have a clear understanding of other great teachers.

So yes, I have accepted Jesus Christ as my teacher, counselor, friend, guide, and savior. Thus, when puzzling or undesirable situations and circumstances arise, a very important question comes to mind: *What would Jesus do?* I "try Jesus," in other words. The results I achieve when I "try Jesus" have taught me that there is an answer to every question, a solution to every problem, and a path to the fulfillment of every goal, need, or desire.

You see, Jesus gave us techniques and principles to live by so that we could live a full and abundant life. And when we live by those techniques, life *is* abundant and full. Yes, there may be valleys just as surely as there are peaks. Still, when we follow the model Jesus set for us, we realize that there is another dimension for us, a spiritual dimension that allows us to look beyond appearances and know that we can overcome any obstacle by following the way Jesus showed us.

Jesus Shows the Way

At the Last Supper when Jesus was bidding the disciples farewell and instructing them to continue following Him, Thomas expressed the fear they all held: "Lord, we do not know where you are going; how can we know the way?" Jesus answered, "I am the way, and the truth, and the life; no one comes to the Father, but by me" (John 14:5–6).

Notice that Jesus did not ask us or the disciples to *worship* Him. We choose to do that. We tend to forget that Jesus was in this world to teach, to heal, to bless, and to be a model for us to *follow*. Jesus was able to perform His great works because the Father empowered Him to do so. The God that was in Jesus is the same God that is in us, and is the one who empowers us to take control of our lives.

I am a firm believer that Jesus was the Wayshower, the model for each of us to follow. As He explained to the disciples, if we know Him, then we automatically know the way to the Father, which is also the way to the Truth and to Life. This, then, is the first thing we should understand about the meaning of "Try Jesus." Jesus is our perfect model. If we accept His words as true and accept His life as the perfect example, then we have at our disposal the means to teach, heal, and bless ourselves and others in our daily activities.

What are some of the examples we can learn from the life of Jesus? Three of the most important ones are *giving thanks, withholding judgment,* and *forgiving.* These are the secrets to living a happy life. I will use the Bible to illustrate these examples and others. Although there are many sources on the life of Jesus Christ, the Bible is a central part of my ministry. I believe every person, every place, and every event in the Bible is symbolic of the various stages of awareness we experience as our lives unfold physically, mentally, emotionally, and spiritually.

1. In All Things Give Thanks

Take a moment right now to close your eyes and say, *Thank You, Father; thank You, Father; thank You, Father!*

What were you thanking Him for? That you have a conscious mind with which you can make choices? That you are surrounded by the abundance of the universe? That your affairs, mind, and body are in God's keeping and safe from all harm? That there is some good thing waiting to come into your life? Yes, you can thank Him for all that and more, for you have so much for which to be thankful. Even if you feel your life this very moment is bleak and without purpose, remember: God is. And for that alone we can all be thankful.

The point is, we don't have to wait until something *specific* happens in order to give thanks. Instead, we should learn to live with an *attitude* of thanksgiving, knowing that whether or not we are aware of it at any given moment, there is always *something* in our lives for which to be thankful. Keeping ourselves poised in thanksgiving keeps us ever ready to receive our blessings.

Jesus understood this principle, and on many occasions He demonstrated how it worked. In the Book of Mark, we read about the feeding of the thousands who had been following Jesus and listening to His teachings for three days. Their food had run out and Jesus was concerned that if He sent them away hungry, some of them would faint on the long journey home. The disciples could see no solution, since they themselves had only seven loaves of bread and a few small fish (Mark 8:1–10).

Jesus knows that we are the children of a merciful Father whose will it is for us to have all that we need.

In the story, Jesus "took the seven loaves and *having given thanks,* broke them and gave them to His disciples . . ." He didn't wait until each man, woman, and child had food in hand before He said "thank you." No, He gave thanks *before* the meal was distributed. Why? Because He knew that the Father would work *through* Him if He opened Himself up and became a channel for that mighty, miracle-working force.

So it is with each of us. We are channels, you and I, for God's work. It is our responsibility to be *open* channels, being ever watchful for ways in which we can do God's will in our own lives or in the lives of others. We cannot fulfill this responsibility, though, if our minds are closed to the possibility of the unexpected. This is what the saying "Expect a miracle" means. Maintain an attitude of thanksgiving and constantly expect God to manifest His goodness in your life.

2. Judge Not and You Will Not Be Judged

I once read in a newspaper that a woman in Oklahoma was put out of her church by three ministers and the chairman of the deacon board. These men cited all the things they had done for the woman. Instead of being grateful (in other words, instead of acting the way they wanted her to act), she had made a mockery of them and the church, they said, by committing fornication. So incensed by the woman's actions were the churchmen that they mailed some 6,000 letters about her throughout the city, including to her place of employment. Everywhere the woman went, someone knew who she was and what she was accused of.

Does this modern-day story remind you of an older one? Yes, it is the familiar story of the woman whom the scribes and the Pharisees brought before Jesus for judgment of her adultery. This modern-day persecution of the church member is but a reenactment of a situation Jesus confronted.

The accusers said to Jesus, "Teacher, this woman has been caught in the act of adultery. Now, in the law, Moses commanded us to stone such. What do you say about her?" Jesus knew that He was continually being tested. Jealous of Him, misunderstanding His mission, the Pharisees were always trying to trap Jesus so that they could discredit Him. How shocked they must have been when Jesus calmly replied, "Let him who is without sin among you be the first to throw a stone at her." He bent to the ground, as He had done when they first put the question to Him, and scribbled something in the dirt with His finger.

To outward appearances, Jesus seemed indifferent to the accusers as He occupied Himself with whatever He was writing. Actually, He was simply giving the Pharisees and the crowd time to think about what they were saying and what they were about to do. After a few moments He looked up. Before Him stood only the woman, her accusers having slipped away one by one (John 8:4–9).

This story has two important messages for us. One: that regardless of the image the world holds of us, there is not one of us who is without sin of some kind. Two: that because we all have done, said, or thought things that may not have been representative of our best or wisest behavior, we owe it to each other to be charitable and compassionate about the secret sins and the public ones with which we all must live.

Judging Ourselves and Others

Jesus had much to say about our judging of one another. In the Sermon on the Mount he told his listeners, "Judge not, and you will not be judged; condemn not, and you will not be condemned" (Luke 6:37). Understand that withholding judgment and condemnation is no guarantee that your fellow humans will not judge and condemn you, for there will always be Pharisees among us. What Jesus is telling us here is that if we refrain from judging our fellow humans, we will not have to suffer that same judgment at our *own* hands.

You've heard the saying "You can't hide from yourself." That is *so* true, for you are the best record keeper of your own deeds, and ultimately **you and you alone must take responsibility for all that you say, think, and do.** Some religions teach that it is God who judges us. However, metaphysics teaches us that God is within each of us, which means that we are our own judges. Once we come to understand this, we can never again say, "So-and-so made me do it," for God gave us free will and the spiritual faculties of judgment and wisdom so that we can take responsibility for our own actions.

Social Differences

Another kind of judgment that Jesus taught us to rise above is judging people on the basis of social differences. There is the instance when Jesus was having dinner with His followers. Among the many people who dined with Him and His disciples that evening were tax collectors and known sinners. Naturally the Pharisees had something to say about this. They wouldn't confront Jesus, though. Instead, they said to His disciples, "Why does your teacher eat with tax collectors and sinners?" Jesus, when told what the Pharisees had said, responded that He had come "not to call the *righteous,* but sinners" (Matthew 9:10–13).

What can we learn from this incident? The psychological term *association brings on assimilation* suggests that we become like those with whom we associate. In metaphysics we also teach that you draw to you that which your thoughts dwell on. So it is right, in the words of Philippians 4:8, that we think on those things that are lovely and of good report. Likewise, it does us good to be around people who are lovely and of good report.

Nevertheless, in this story we see that Jesus did not shun the people who sought Him out simply because they were of a lower social order or because they were known to be sinners. As He said, "Those who are well have not need of a physician." In other words, He knew Himself to be a blessing to those who sought Him out. By the same token, might not each of us be a blessing to those who seek us out or those in whose company we find ourselves? If that is our role in such a person's life—to be a blessing—then we can only fulfill it by withholding judgment of that person.

Looking Beyond Appearances

There also are times when people we care for or admire do not behave up to their potential. Perhaps they are "letting themselves go" in one way or another. Perhaps they are displaying undesirable personality traits or are following a lifestyle that can only lead to physical, social, mental, or spiritual collapse. They are, in other words, not expressing the Christ of themselves, not living according to what is best in their nature and according to what is in their best interest.

What do you do? Certainly you do not judge. You *under-stand,* but you do not judge, condemn, or verbally attack. Here is an opportunity for you to "Try Jesus!" Love the Christ in your friend, even though you don't love what the person is doing or the situation the person is in. Look beyond appearances and affirm in your mind: *I know that if* (name of your friend) *would move just a little farther along the path, she would know this kind of behavior isn't necessary. Instead of condemning, I behold and love the Christ in her and I see her acting for her highest good.*

The important thing to remember about judging others is that we are all working out our own salvation. You are working out yours; I am working out mine. We never know exactly why a person does a given thing or acts a certain way. Every action is the effect of a cause or a series of causes that accumulate in the mind and heart of the doer and manifest in the end result we see. But, as Jesus said, "Do not judge by appearances, but judge with right judgment" (John 7:24). If we judge with right judgment, we will not attack or condemn anyone else's personal life, because there is probably enough in our own lives that requires our attention and judgment!

3. Forgive and You Will Be Forgiven

Probably the thing that slows our spiritual growth most is lack of forgiveness. When He first spoke what we now call The Lord's Prayer, Jesus explained just one section of the prayer: "For if you forgive men their trespasses," He said, "your heavenly Father also will forgive you; but if you do not forgive men their trespasses, neither will your Father forgive your trespasses" (Matthew 6:14–15).

In the Lord's Prayer, then, Jesus shows us the way to a

greater consciousness and spiritual growth. The way to this greater consciousness is to ask for forgiveness each day ("forgive us our debts") and to be forgiving in turn ("as we have also forgiven our debtors") (Matthew 6:12).

Forgiveness is an important theme in the teachings of Jesus. Throughout the Scriptures we find Him forgiving those whom He has healed, instructing the disciples to forgive those who wrong them, instructing the persecuted to love their enemies. And as He was nailed to the cross, rather than condemn those responsible for the act, He said, "Father, forgive them; for they know not what they do" (Luke 23: 34). Do you see why I say Jesus was the perfect example, the perfect model for us to follow?

The Importance of Forgiveness

Why is forgiving such an important act? Well, to answer that, let's consider what goes on in the heart and mind of a person who is holding on to some real or imagined injustice. First, the injustice itself continues to live in the person's mind just as though it happened five minutes ago. All the details— what the other person said, how the remarks made the injured person feel, what kinds of consequences the injured person had to face following the injustice—everything is right there in vivid, instant replay. This means that the painful experience continues to live in today's reality, taking up mental and emotional space that could be given to more uplifting and productive thoughts.

This is not a healthy state of mind, for anything that lives makes demands on the environment in which it lives. Plants constantly take nutrients from the soil in which they grow; living things continuously take oxygen from the air; parasites take what they need from their host, whether the host is willing or not.

Even electrical appliances deplete the source from which they derive the energy needed to operate. Living ideas and thoughts are the same way. They must obtain energy from somewhere in order to flourish. Therefore, **it is wise to be sure that every thought that we allow to draw from our energy is a thought that will pay us back in harmony, productivity, happiness, and general well-being.** Thoughts of resentment or plans to "get even" do not contribute to us in any useful way. Instead, they steal valuable reserves of energy that could be put to better use in advancing our spiritual, physical, intellectual, and emotional well-being.

Jesus knew this, and so He took every opportunity to advise His followers to clear their minds and hearts of the debris of hard feelings. The Father also wants us to maintain a healthy mental and spiritual environment. That something within you which prompts you to do a little more when you're tired, to improve on a job already well done, to listen to a troubled person when you've got troubles of your own—that's the Christ within, the God-self of you urging you to let divinity be your guiding force.

When you have not forgiven someone, the better part of your human nature is troubled by your refusal to be forgiving. You feel it—you know you do! When you continue to harbor ill feelings and be unforgiving, something in you says, "I really should forget about this," or "I really should apologize to so-and-so." There is something within that *knows* better and will not "give you a break" until you *act* better. This, then, is the meaning of "if you do not forgive men their trespasses, neither will your Father forgive your trespasses."

What are you holding on to that you should release? Whatever it is, don't let it continue to stand in the way of your good. Remember, your mind can supply energy to harmful as well as beneficial thoughts. Why not demand that every thought you give energy to shall be a beneficial one?

My Forgiveness List with Affirmations

Forgiveness is an inner act that one takes to clear up negativity in one's consciousness. As long as you entertain an unforgiving thought, your outer behavior reflects your inner belief. Your body language will further demonstrate your attitude. It is good to make a list of persons, organizations, situations, experiences of the past and present that need to be forgiven. I find that writing your list or using a letter form is most beneficial. If you need to, send the letter to the person. Otherwise burn it. In burning the letter, it becomes the nothingness that the situation is anyway and the healing takes place.

1. List or write a letter to the people you now forgive. This may cause you some pain, but until you face the pain you cannot gain release. Until you forgive, your pain intensifies itself. In the body it can produce an unhealthy condition.

   I now forgive you and release you to your highest good, freeing us to peace and harmony now.

2. List or write a letter to all whom you desire to forgive you.

   I am open and receptive to your forgiveness of me, releasing me to my highest good and freeing us to peace and harmony now.

   Transformation is change. In order to establish a forgiveness technique from which you will benefit: **Before you retire at night forgive everyone who has caused you some mental or emotional challenge for the day.** This also includes you too. Isaiah 55:11: "So shall my word be that goeth forth: it shall not return unto me void, but it shall accomplish that which I please and it shall prosper in the thing whereto I sent it."

Every word we speak goes into the ethers and reaches those for whom we are concerned.

CHAPTER SIX

✳

Turn Your Water into Wine

The Scriptures tell us that "There is a spirit in man, and the breath of the Almighty giveth him understanding" (Job 32:8). The only way you are going to know this Spirit is to act as though you believe It is there. Talk to It. Talk to It in Truth, talk to It in Love, talk to It in Light. Once you get in the habit of talking to Spirit, you will find that not only is It a good listener but that It answers you and does indeed make you understand.

One thing Spirit can make you understand is that you are not a powerless victim of circumstances. If something goes wrong or if there is not enough of some good thing in your life, *you have within you the force that will change the circumstances for your highest good.* Jesus knew this Truth and demonstrated it time after time. Since human consciousness brings forth many experiences of lack and limitation, let us examine the first time Jesus demonstrated the Truth of changing circumstances by performing a miracle. This miracle was the restoring of the wine supply at a wedding.

The Miracle of the Wine

On the third day there was a marriage at Cana in Galilee, and the mother of Jesus was there. Jesus also was invited to the marriage, with His disciples. When the wine gave out, Jesus' mother said to Him, "They have no wine." And Jesus said to her, "O woman, what have you to do with me? My hour has not yet come." His mother said to the servants, "Do whatever He tells you."

Six stone jars were standing there for the Jewish rites of purification. Each could hold twenty or thirty gallons of water. Jesus said to them, "Fill the jars with water." And they filled them up to the brim. He said to them, "Now draw some out and take it to the steward of the feast." So they took it.

When the steward of the feast tasted the water, now become wine, and did not know where it came from (though the servants who had drawn the water knew), the steward of the feast called the bridegroom and said to him, "Every man serves the good wine first; and when men have drunk freely, then the poor wine; but you have kept the good wine until now" (John 2:1–10).

Be in Control of Yourself

I have to laugh about this situation because, really, nothing has changed. Consciousness repeats itself. People today who call themselves "partying" do the same thing. They drink up the best and then, when everybody's out of control, they bring out the rest. This is another reason why *you must always be in control of yourself.* Any time you are out of control, you're in trouble. **You need always to be mindful of who you are, what's happening to you, and also of what's going into your body at any given time.**

As I said at the beginning of this chapter, you are not a helpless victim of circumstances, but losing control of yourself can turn you into such a person. When you are in control of yourself, you are in control of your words, thoughts, actions, and reactions. This means that *you* make the decision when to stop or start doing something for your own good; *you* decide how you will react to things that have the potential to be upsetting; *you* decide how you will feel about the things that go on in your life.

This being in control of yourself is a real responsibility, in other words. It requires constantly being tuned in to who you are—a child of God. There are things that you will or will not do when you have this consciousness. And this consciousness helps you direct your life so that it is in keeping with the best you can experience. Responsibility, yes—but the reward is well worth the effort.

One responsibility you have is to **determine what you want your life to be like.** That's right. Make the determination for yourself. Don't just haphazardly pass through your days, letting things happen as they may. True, there is a certain amount of "going with the flow" that you must learn to do. This is what we mean by "Let go and let God." But that *going with* the flow must be balanced with your use of judgment and wisdom to *create* a flow that leads you ever onward toward the unfoldment of the best that you can be. Part of creating your own flow has to do with believing that you *can* share in the abundance of the universe. You *can* have both water and wine.

How Much Wine Do You Want?

You may think that the usefulness of the principles Jesus taught stopped with the disciples. You may feel, "That was for those people; that's not for me." But there was no time frame around what Jesus taught. His teachings would not have survived all these years if they had been good for only a certain period of time. Furthermore, His teachings will continue to survive, because His message is eternal.

The question, then, is not "Can you too turn water into wine?" The question is, *"How much wine do you want?"* (I am speaking metaphysically, of course. If at some point you turn physical water into physical wine, please write me at once!)

The Revealing Word, a religious dictionary, says that wine "symbolizes the vitality that forms the connecting link between soul and body." In defining water, it states: "In one of its aspects, it represents negativeness. The individual who allows himself to become negative to the good finds himself uncertain and unstable in his mind, and often becomes so submerged in the waters of negation that his physical condition is low."

We know from teachings and from experience that negation can result in a poor physical condition as well as a poor emotional or psychological condition; which, in turn, can lead to a general lack of fulfillment in all areas of our lives. At such times, what we want to do is to turn the water of negation into the wine of vitality.

Now, let's put these concepts and definitions "on hold" for a moment and lay some groundwork for using them further.

When There Needs to Be a Miracle

You know, it is truly amazing how things happen in our lives at a time when there needs to be a miracle. At any given moment, without warning, something can happen in our lives or in the life of someone close to us, something for which the only solution is a miracle. We've all had experiences of this kind. For example, the car suddenly stops running and you have no money to have it repaired; plans that you have had for a long time are thrown out of kilter because someone failed to do something as promised; you've spent all of your money, and here comes that "deferred payment" bill you forgot you were to start paying this month. Anything can happen. So it was at the wedding feast. When Jesus arrived with His mother, they had run out of wine.

I don't know if during Jesus' growth as a child, Mary, as mothers will do, had noticed some special things that made her call to Jesus' attention that the wine had run out. There is no Scripture to tell us what experiences Mary had as a mother, except that she knew at the time of conception that He was called the Son of God. At the wedding, it seems as though she is being a typical mother who has a very beautiful son. No matter who we are, if we are mothers we always think our children are special. So the minute the wine ran out, Mary jumped right up and said, "C'mon, now, Son. Show them what you can do." Aren't all parents this way?

Whether or not this is what Mary was demonstrating, Jesus spoke very sharply to her: "O woman, what have you to do with me? My hour has not yet come." Some people feel that Jesus was being rude to His mother. He was not. The Jewish custom of address to all females was "woman." Jesus was not being "sassy," as some would call it. He simply addressed her according to the custom of the time.

So, no, there was no rudeness in Jesus' answer. He wasn't angry, either. He preached happiness and abundance, so He surely didn't want the wedding feast to be disrupted. If anything, He was probably just surveying the situation to decide "How much wine do they *need*?" Is there a lesson there for us? Of course there is!

Stay Calm

The second part of Jesus' response, "My hour has not yet come," is extremely important because it reminds us that Jesus was teaching a *process*. We worship Jesus; we love Jesus. However, we forget to see the *process* that He gave us to follow so that we can bless, heal, and multiply.

The first thing we can learn about the process Jesus used in turning this water into wine is: **When you meet a need in your life, don't panic; stay calm.** Jesus did not get ruffled. When He told Mary, "My hour has not yet come," He was doing His inner work. He knew what He had to do to demonstrate the power, the miracle-working power. So, when something comes into your experience, before you start running, before you start trying to figure a way out, get still and do your prayer work.

How would you respond if your employer said to you tomorrow, "We won't be needing you anymore"? Would these thoughts rise up in you: "How am I going to make ends meet?" "How am I going to pay the children's tuition?" "There goes the vacation!" Fear thoughts such as these can leave you in a real panic. Instead of giving way to fears at such times, slow yourself down long enough to say something like this:

> *Okay, God, just help me to get myself calmed down, because I know You brought this opportunity and You can always bring another. When one door closes, another one can open. But I'm the one who has to see to it, because You have already done what You're going to do. You are just waiting*

on me to act like I know that You are God and besides You,
there is no other. So, if this situation doesn't work out, You
have many ways I know not of to make another situation
work for my highest good.

Prosperity and the Wine of Life

Now let's go back to the lesson contained in *The Revealing Word* and its definitions of water and wine. It said that water, in one of its aspects, represents negativeness and that we sometimes become so negative that we are submerged in the waters of negation. In this state of negativeness, it would not be unusual to find ourselves short on prosperity of some kind.

I want us to be clear that when we use the word *prosperity,* we're talking about health. We are talking about peace of mind—a sense of well-being. We are also talking about what most often comes to mind at the mention of prosperity—financial, material, and social stability. In other words, we are talking about *all the wealth, all the goodness that God is.* When we recognize that prosperity covers all of these areas of our lives, we will begin to realize that it must have a spiritual basis. Prosperity brings vitality, the wine of life.

We need to be clear on something else; Jesus did not condemn wealth. No, He didn't! He condemned *the way we misuse wealth,* how we attach to it ideas of cheating, of lying, of working undercover to obtain wealth.

Actually Jesus provided a good example of prosperity in action. He had twelve men with Him almost constantly. Yet they never suffered, they were never hungry. Jesus ate with the best. He wore a seamless robe. He even had a treasurer, Judas, so they must have had some substance coming through in some way.

Jesus Taught Prosperity

The disciples were ordinary working people, like you and me—fishermen, tax collectors, and so forth. They gave up their livelihoods to follow Jesus. In return, He taught them the first prosperity principle: **Trust in the presence and the power of God, and you cannot suffer;** "Seek first the kingdom of God and His righteousness and all manner of good things will be added unto you" (Matthew 6:33).

In teaching the disciples, Jesus taught us too. You don't have to beat anybody over the head and take their money; you don't have to invest in quick-money schemes. None of that has to be done, because *God is the source.* The challenge we have is that everybody wants "theirs" right now. There is a side of us that says, "Whatever you are going to do, do it now!" We are in a hurry; we are running here and there.

The result of all this hurrying is that we get very confused about the source of our prosperity. If we are in a financial bind and we can't get a loan from the bank or a friend or a relative, we think we're finished. Is this what Jesus taught? Is this what God promised? I don't think so. These attitudes are examples of putting money above God, and that is what Jesus condemned.

We must recognize that *money is an earthly expression of God.* If we didn't have money, don't you think God has the intelligence to bring forward another idea for some form of exchange? Those of us who go way back remember the time when money was scarce and people used all kinds of things as forms of exchange. Preachers were paid with Sunday dinners, doctors were paid with chickens and eggs, laborers were paid with shelter from the elements. There has always been a way to express God's will of prosperity for all.

So, returning to the first step in the process of the water-to-wine miracle, if you find yourself in a situation where some part of your prosperity is threatened, your first step is to *stay calm*. You can accomplish nothing by giving in to panic and fear. At such times, you don't think straight, you don't express yourself clearly, you don't maintain a sense of how things *can* work out if you will *let* them work out.

I can't repeat it often enough—*stay calm*. Don't give way to panic and fear.

Praise and Use What You Have

At the wedding, the calming step for Jesus was almost instantaneous. Jesus told the servants to fill the jars with water. When the servants filled these twenty- or thirty-gallon jars to the brim, they held 120 to 180 gallons. These were just ordinary stone pots.

Someone probably wondered why He didn't send for wine bottles; why would He use these old stone water pots? What Jesus was demonstrating was the need to get in the habit of taking what we have in hand right at any given time and then loving it, praising it, blessing it. The second step of the process, then, is **praise what you have and use it.**

If you have only one penny in your pocket as you read this book, praise and give thanks for that penny as you know the Truth about it. It is but a tiny symbol of the abundance that awaits you. If you don't have anything in your wallet or purse, praise and give thanks that you've got a wallet or purse to put something in, because God promises that if you trust Him, He will fill it to the brim.

In other words, despite appearances, you are never separated from your good. If there appears to be a separation, it has its origins in your mind—remember the law of cause and effect. You can eliminate the separation by eliminating the thoughts

that led to it. **Replace those thoughts with thoughts of good
flowing to you and running over.**

So, in keeping with this principle, Jesus had the servants fill
the old water pots. Those old pots represent the conditions we
face every day. For instance, many young people in need of an
education are just throwing up their hands and saying, "Well,
the government is cutting off this and that, and so there's no
need for me to even try to go to school." What they fail to
realize is that the government doesn't control their *minds*. Rather
than adopt this defeatist attitude, they need to believe that there
is a power greater than any action anybody can take from upstairs
or miles away. Many of us came through school without any
government benefits, and we made it.

What about the specific problem you are facing today? Are
you giving up too fast? Are you allowing your intellect to have
control and not your Spirit? Think about it! What is it that
you're facing today? Are you loving it, so that you can see the
good that is there?

Problem = Challenge = Opportunity

Always remember that *challenges come to show us a new way.*
In every challenge, there is good. However, if you give up too
easily, then you have not given yourself an opportunity to learn
what there is in the challenge for you to learn. That is why
someone said that *problems are opportunities. Each problem you solve
is a step forward in your growth.* This doesn't mean that we need
to go out looking for problems, but neither does it mean that
we should fold up and quit seeking the good when problems
appear.

The filling of the old water pots at the wedding, then,
means *take what you have and start there.* Ask the Father for direction as to where to go from that point. Don't panic. Just go

within and talk to the Father. You've got to **take what you have, bless it, praise it, and use it.**

Thank God for Answered Prayer

While the servants filled the water pots, you can be sure that Jesus continued to bless the situation. When the pots were filled, He said to the servants, "Now draw some out, and take it to the steward of the feast." This tells us that once you have worked through the first two steps, you begin thanking God for answered prayer. In every miracle that Jesus performed, He acted as though the miracle was already accomplished even as He was in the process of performing the miracle. This is where your faith comes in, to believe that what you have prayed for is being done even as you are praying.

Realize that when Jesus performed miracles and acted as if they were already accomplished before they came into manifestation, He was taking a stand on negativity. How many times have you been striving to accomplish something, only to have "friends" say to you, "It'll never work!" And if your "friends" will say this to you, think how much more negativity is out there waiting to "zap" you!

Cancel All Negatives

This is why it is important that you never show the least bit of doubt about what you set out to do. Act confidently, and people who notice you during your period of waiting or working toward your goal will be infected by your confidence. If you act doubtful or uncertain, you simply invite others to put their doubt or uncertainty into words. Knowing what you know now about the power of the word, you certainly don't want anyone speaking negative words over your miracles!

Also, it is important for you to cancel any negative words *you* might accidentally speak. For instance, if you feel the need to confide in someone as you are working to accomplish something, in the process of confiding, you might unintentionally give voice to your own doubts.

(Some people do this intentionally, hoping that the listener will talk them out of the doubts. It is better to talk yourself out of your doubts.) If this happens, be sure that you end each statement of doubt with a statement of faith. You might identify the problems you see, but always counteract those problems by saying, "It's in Divine Order," or words to that effect.

It Will Come—In Abundance

Returning to the parable, then, the steward, not knowing where the wine had come from, said to the bridegroom, "Every man serves the good wine first; and when men have drunk freely, then the poor wine; but you have kept the good wine until now." What does that tell us? It says that **no matter how long you may have to wait for your good, when it comes, it will always come in abundance.**

At Hillside we had been working many years toward the building of a circular sanctuary. I was often asked, "When are you going to get the church up?" My answer was, "We have that idea in mind; and when it comes, when the door really opens, when the money flows in, *it is going to come in abundance.*"

People of a like mind understood my answer. For instance, one evening after a meeting I was talking to Reverend Martin Luther King, Sr. (now deceased) as he sat in his wheelchair waiting for his car. I asked how he was, and he said, "Fine, fine. How's the church coming along?" I told him we were working, consciously working toward the day of building. He replied,

"Baby, try to build the church debt-free. Build it debt-free. Don't have all that interest, don't have your people tied up for years." I appreciated that statement because it was another idea coming from the Father; I said, "Thank you, God."

Just wait and be persistent in your waiting, even when it doesn't seem like the answer is there; *perhaps it just isn't time for it to be revealed to you.* Your job is to keep trusting. During the time you are waiting, you can prove the Lord, because you can keep your faith through prayer, meditation, and affirmation.

If You Want Wine, Think *Wine*

Always keep in mind the vision of your desired outcome. If you want wine, think wine. Remember, your outer experience produces the likeness of the seed planted in your subconscious.

You *can* turn your water into wine. But before you can accomplish this miracle you must understand that God's will for His people is all good. The way to gain this understanding is to begin to build consciously the Truths of God. You've got to build these Truths in your mind. They become your reservoir. When you consciously believe that God is the source of your supply, you subconsciously begin to feel it. Remember, the subconscious is the doer. Whatever you consciously give your subconscious, you will experience.

Work in the Kingdom Within

That's how God works. Jesus told us that the kingdom of heaven was at hand. Don't look around for it; it is *within you.* This kingdom is the realm of divine ideas, for everything that is seen had first to be an idea in somebody's mind. So praise God for this Truth!

Jesus, through His miracles, through His parables, through His promises, let us know that if we would take the steps—if we would follow the commandments, *if we would mentally live by His laws*—we would have the outer experience to show for what is taking place on the inside. There can be no visibility unless you first work with the invisible. That's the thing with which you are going to have to begin: the invisible. Recognize that everything takes place from within before it becomes an outer manifestation.

So when you look at the aspects of prosperity, when you look at your finances in particular, you must understand that *money is a part of God* and that God has brought that gift to you for you to use wisely. That is why you always have to use your faculty of understanding. Ask God for wisdom, for judgment in knowing *how* to do, *what* to do, *when* to do, and then follow through when you get that leading.

You Will Be Led

There will be a period of waiting after you ask for guidance. During that waiting period, a good situation may seem completely out of whack. This is just the time when you need to keep yourself in tune with God, to know that when God tells you to move, it is divine timing. This is divine right action, and the manifestation of it will always be for your highest good. So during this time, let go of anxiety, let go of worry. Whatever the situation, know that you do not have to carry it out yourself. Remember there is a presence, that comes to you as a thought, a hunch, a nudging—that something within. I like to believe this "something within" is God.

To every problem, there is always the perfect answer. The

desire and the desired are one. God, in His mighty wisdom, is the Source, the Provider of every good and perfect gift. He promised never to leave you and even sent His son, Jesus Christ, that you might live life and live it more abundantly.

AFFIRMATIONS

1. *God is the source of my supply, I am never without money (health, friends).*
2. *I can do all things through Christ who strengthens me.*
3. *I am the rich child of a loving God who desires to give me the kingdom of happiness, joy and every good thing.*
4. *I give thanks that God is the source of my talents, my blessings, and my expressions.*
5. *I give thanks that I am a child in whom God is well pleased.*
6. *I give thanks that God sent His son, Jesus Christ, to show me the way.*
7. *God's love and protection free me from every thought of fear, and I am strong and well.*
8. *Divine love is now working through me to adjust all the details of my life.*
9. *I am a mighty magnet for good, to flow from within to attract good from without.*
10. *God's love in us is drawing to us new ideas, new courage, and visible daily supply.*
11. *God is my protection.*
12. *God's perfect harmony and perfect peace is doing its perfect work in me—right now!*

CHAPTER SEVEN

*

Relationships

Everybody Wants to Be Loved, Nobody Wants to Love!

$\mathcal{A}$s a pastor, I find that counseling falls into three major areas: health, finance, and relationships. We talk about health and finance in chapters ten and eleven. Relationships cover a broad territory. There are those who feel unloved, some who feel unworthy of love. There are men and women who want to get married to others, who want harmony and understanding in a marriage relationship. There are parents who reject their sons and daughters who are gay and lesbian. There are lonely people who want friends and companionship. There are those who feel no one understands them, that they are unneeded and unwanted. All of the above constitute relationships. Relationships begin with how one relates to one's self.

It has often been said that if you want to know the "consciousness" of our nation, check the best-sellers in the bookstores. I would add to this, check the self-help sections of the bookstores. Whatever the book title, relationships are involved.

Talk-show hosts, soap operas, daytime dramas, prime-time TV shows and even the news keep us inundated with programs that can drain us emotionally as we sit and listen to the pain of others throughout the world. Generally, the talk-show hosts provide the participants with trained therapists who aid in their finding solutions to their problems. The average listener can also have a learning experience from the program.

It's the follow-up that is of concern to some of us who are aware that a one-hour Band-Aid is not enough for resolution to a challenge that has most often resulted from a dysfunctional family. Many adults have suffered as children from mental, emotional, or physical abuse and neglect by dysfunctional parents. Dysfunctional family systems produce delusions, compulsivity, frozen feelings, low self-worth, and medical complications. Negative emotions that result include fear, insecurity, feelings of loneliness or desertion, ineffectiveness, anger, guilt, grief and shame. All of the above affect us in our relationship with God, ourselves and others.

You are totally aware by now that this book is based on spiritual principles that have not only helped me in my spiritual growth, but that I believe will be a blessing to you. Jesus was once asked by a rich young ruler, "What must I do to inherit eternal life?" He had kept all the commandments.—Thou shalt not kill; Thou shalt not steal; Thou shalt not lie; etc. . . . Jesus' reply was: *"Thou shalt love the Lord thy God with all thy heart, soul and mind. And the second commandment is like unto it, thou shalt love thy neighbor as thyself"* (Matthew 22:37–39).

It appears that Jesus is saying relationships require God first, ourselves second and others last. Somehow many of us have come to believe we must take care of everybody else and ourselves last. I certainly practiced it through the years until I began to investigate my true relationship with God. I learned my mind is my connecting link with God. Through prayer and meditation I found

out what the Psalmist meant in Psalm 46:7: "Be still and know that
I am God. . . ." We can then experience the power to connect
with others in the same loving, positive way we connect to God.
In fact, I like the word *connect*. That is what we are all about, our
connections with God and with each other. My friend, Father Leo
Booth, author of *Spirituality and Recovery,* puts it this way:

> I consider our relationship with God (as we under-
> stand Him or Her) to be essential, pervasive and the
> key to the discovery of the spiritual life. However, it
> is also my belief that God is manifested in this world,
> in creation, in people. If we do not develop a rela-
> tionship with ourselves, if we do not embark on the
> journey into self, then I do not believe we can com-
> prehend the reality of God in the universe.

As the highest form of creation made in the spiritual image-
likeness of God, we know that God as Spirit works through us
as we choose to allow ourselves to be channels of love and compassion.

The Apostle Paul in the thirteenth chapter of 1 Corinthians,
verses 4–7, gives to us a treatise on Love:

> Love is very patient and kind, never jealous or envi-
> ous, never boastful or proud, never haughty or selfish
> or rude. Love does not demand its own way. It is not
> irritable or touchy. It does not hold grudges and will
> hardly even notice when others do it wrong. It is
> never glad about injustice, but rejoices whenever truth
> wins out. If you love someone you will be loyal to
> him no matter what the cost. You will always believe
> in him, always expect the best of him, and always stand
> your ground in defending him.

The question then becomes, How do I make this self-discovery of love in me now that I know what love is and what love is not? How will this help me to understand self-love so I can begin practicing my true self to better my relationship with spouses, lovers, family, friends, coworkers and people whom I meet daily from every walk of life? Self-love is discovering the greatness deep within you, knowing you are a beloved child of God, knowing that within you resides the Spirit of God, knowing that you are a spiritual being having a spiritual experience in a spiritual universe. Self-love is experiencing God at work in you, through you and around you, thus making you an open channel for the healing energy of love (spirit) to be expressed first in you and then to others. Self-love is a deep sense of self-esteem, self-worth, self-respect, self-dignity, honesty, pride in ourself caused by an abiding faith and belief in God.

Today we are aware that God has many names. For some it is simply "my Higher Power." We have learned scientifically of the Quantum Theory that there is something very real and undefinable in the universe. I call it God, Father-Mother God. Most of us generally say, "something told me."

With all of the above, what is our next step in improving and beginning new relationships?

I. Love God First

Love God above all else. As children of God we are endowed with power. Our ministry celebrates the power of God in us as faith, strength, love, wisdom, power, will, understanding, zeal, order, renunciation and life. *"My beloved, now are we the sons of God"* (1 John 3:2). We understand God to be an Intelligence and a Presence, not a person. Jesus established His relationship with God when teaching His disciples to pray, using the words "our Father." In our relationships with each other, we are all created by one Creator. There is unity in all people and in all life; therefore, we are all expressions of the One God. God did not choose any particular race, creed or color; we choose God. When we are aware of this truth we can begin to see relationships extending to all of humankind. Jesus' mission was one of love and to establish our personal relationship to the creator.

II. Love Ourselves Second

1. Take care of your body. Paul admonishes us that the body is the temple of the Holy Spirit. It needs good nutrition, exercise and love. Hug yourself daily and tell your body (spiritual substance in shape and form) how much you love and care for it. Simply call your name as you hug your body and say, "I love you." The results are rewarding as you appreciate the life of God in you.

2. Be positive about yourself. Self-criticism and self-condemnation strip you of your joy and happiness as a human being. I have been a tall person since I was thirteen (six feet five inches in my stocking feet). For a very long time I didn't like me. I pretended to be okay, was active in school and community activities, was an honor roll student, and led a busy adult life. I cried daily and asked God, "Why me?" With the spiritual principles of Jesus Christ I turned the "why me" into "why *not* me" and began a process of personal transformation that I am still growing in and enjoying today. Find something positive to say about yourself daily. It helps you to feel good about yourself. It stops you from being concerned about what others think, especially when it's negative.

3. Allow others to support you. This may be through counseling services, a support group, or close friends who allow you to be yourself without criticism. We all need the love and support of others no matter what it is we are doing in our lives. As a minister I've learned to keep a small group of close friends around me to whom I can express my concerns, cry, and shout good news as well. They understand I am a spiritual being (first) having a human experience. I recommend that when you are seeking guidance go to God first and then go to others as God directs you. There are some professionally trained counselors and therapists who can help you to find answers. Many churches offer spiritual counseling, as we do at Hillside. Personally, I am a member of a co-dependency support group, which helps me in not neglecting my own identity as I work with others.

4. Be patient with yourself. When things don't move fast enough or there are appearances of failure, don't blow a fuse. Slow down and become centered again through a quiet time of meditation. Sometimes a quiet place may not be available, but there is within you your own sanctuary to which you can retreat. Simply repeating "Peace" can bring you back to knowing that no matter what the appearance or outcome, all is in divine order. There are so many times we allow ourselves the pleasure of worrying, being upset over things we cannot change. Every experience has good in it, a lesson to be learned.

5. Express thanksgiving for everything whether it is great or small. I recently heard a speaker say, "Americans have forgotten how to say excuse me, please, and thank you." I agree wholeheartedly. I work with parents in our ministry in these areas as part of parenting skills with their children. However, adults need to remember to be thankful as well. Giving thanks increases our opportunity to receive more. In biblical times the Psalmists in

the Book of Psalms were always thanking and praising God for His goodness. The prophets of the Old Testament and Jesus of the New Testament proved the power of giving thanks. Paul the Apostle said, *"In every thing give thanks."* Iyanla Vanzant has produced a book titled *Acts of Faith, Daily Meditations for People of Color*. The November 24 lesson sums it all up for people of any color:

> Can you see, hear and speak? Can you walk, move around and do things for yourself? Did you eat today? Yesterday? Someday last week? Can you pick up a telephone? Turn on a light? Stick a key in a door and have a place to sleep? Are your feet adequately covered? Do you have something to wear? Are your lungs and kidneys functioning? Can you breathe without assistance? Can you move your hands, arms, legs and do the things you want to do? Is there someone who will help you if you need help? Is there someone from whom you receive love? Is there someone you know who will be there no matter what you've done? Can you laugh when you want to? Cry if you need to? Does your mind let you know the difference between the two? Is there a tree you can touch? A flower you can smell? Can you stand in the rays of the sun? Give thanks for every "yes" you can give and remind yourself that you are truly blessed.

6. Look into your eyes often. I have found using the mirror in my bathroom to be a wonderful way to express love for myself and my family members. I forgive myself for mistakes of the past. I talk to my aunt and my son to say "I love you." Looking in the mirror is not behaving the same as the wicked stepmother in *Cinderella*, but a way to get in touch with your feelings. There

is a peace that follows when you become aware of your feelings as a result of this exercise.

7. Tell yourself how well you are doing. As I was writing this chapter I responded to the praise I gave myself for listening to God's guidance for what I would say to you the reader. I give praise for learning to listen to my body when it tells me to stop or for waiting for answers when I am humanly anxious. Praise yourself. You deserve to give thanks for you.

8. You deserve the best. Don't wait to get the new job or the new relationship or the new condo—begin now to know that wherever you are you deserve the best. Increase your faith in God and strengthen your prayer life by affirming daily: "God loves me." As you plant this affirmation in the fertile ground of your consciousness it will bring forth abundant fruit. I also found the first verse of the twenty-seventh Psalm to be helpful:

> The Lord is my light and my salvation, whom shall I fear? The Lord is the strength of my life, of whom shall I be afraid?

9. Learn to forgive yourself and others. Forgiveness is an act of love. It is an energy that heals and brings comfort, joy and peace. Where there are unforgiving thoughts there is conflict. Where there is conflict there is no peace. Many relationships become centers of disruption because the people involved will not forgive when others have been thoughtless or unkind.

10. Take time to be still and pray. We are renewed inwardly and filled with strength. We can see things in their true perspective. Meditation helps us to release anxiety and tension. We are able to trust in the love and power of God at work in us.

III. *Loving Others for a Healthier Relationship*

A positive attitude and behavior is the passage to a meaningful relationship with others. In the previous section we learned ways in which we can love ourselves in order to unconditionally love others. Remembering what love is not, as mentioned earlier in 1 Corinthians Chapter 13, you can see that the following characteristics will keep you from reaching out into new areas or engaging in new and different relationships:

1. A superiority complex, egotism, and prejudice.
2. Self-centeredness or narcissism, producing insecurity and immaturity.
3. False pride, bragging, phoniness to impress.
4. "I want what I want, when I want it"—self-will.

Instead, speak honestly about your feelings, be a good listener, accept criticism gracefully, and share with others through gifts of love (flowers, friendship cards, telephone calls). Find time to do volunteer work. This works well for those with life-threatening illnesses who can give back to those who also face diseases. There is a beautiful story in the November 27, 1994, issue of the *Atlanta Constitution,* our daily newspaper, about a rabbi praying for a miracle. He has incurable cancer. Yet he has been an inspiration to his family, his congregation, and to colleagues throughout the country. In May, he was told he'd live only three months—and now it's November. Praise God! His congregation continues to grow, and construction is under way for a youth chapel and classrooms. He continues to give his talent to others. The congregation has responded with their prayers, plants, hugs, conversations and care.

Give and it shall be given unto you good measure, pressed down, shaken together and running over (Luke 6:38).

Volunteering opens doors to meeting and making new friends. Attending the church, synagogue, mosque, or sponsored activities with special interest groups such as Parents Without Partners can help one to develop relationships.

In this I have attempted to give to you the reader the spiritual foundation for relationships that work, whether you are concerned about God, yourself or others. Use this chapter as a measurement to see where you are right now with you! Perhaps this chapter prompts you to read a book on relationships.

In conclusion, work toward balancing your life, and expect every day to be your fullest. Remember, positive relationships don't just happen, but as was stated in chapter one, we must practice the characteristics that make for change in our lives. As you practice loving God, yourself, and others you will attract to you the right person, friend or business associate.

AFFIRMATIONS

1. *Divine love enfolds me and only good can come to me.*

2. *I am a radiating center of Divine love.*

3. *God loves me.*

4. *As I love myself I can express and share love with others.*

5. *The presence of God watches over me and no one can hurt me.*

6. *Divine love is at work in my life now attracting to me my true wife (my true husband).*

7. *I believe there is a man (woman) in the universe waiting to love and marry me.*

8. *The activity of Divine love in me now attracts my perfect soul mate.*

9. *I let the Christ love fill me with understanding and I attract positive, healthy relationships.*

10. *The love of Christ within me gives me the ability to forgive fully and freely.*

11. *The Spirit of the Lord goes before me to make happy and successful my way.*

12. *I deserve to be loved by myself and others.*

13. *I am not alone, I am one with God and the Universe.*

CHAPTER EIGHT

*

Living Single

$\mathcal{T}$oday living single has its joys and its sorrows. It carries with it responsibilities that require a mature mind and positive self-esteem: knowing the frustration of having a roommate who spends their share of the rent before the due date; knowing how to budget; remembering all the dos and don'ts of Mama's advice; being away from home for the first time . . . the list continues. Even when the above experiences are corrected there still seems to be a feeling of being alone. Sororities, fraternities, church singles groups, personal newspaper ads all serve a purpose. Many times one is surrounded by friends, family and coworkers but continues to find difficulty in those moments when they are alone.

In every self-help book there's a chapter on how to overcome loneliness. Some of these books harbor the misconception that women are lonelier than men, but studies have indicated that men and women experience loneliness about equally. Men may not talk of loneliness as much as women do, but it is the same challenge for both male and female.

In coping with loneliness, we must first go back to the truth that life is consciousness. What is consciousness? It's awareness. Whatever you are aware of is what you will express in your everyday life. Also, loneliness is a state of mind that we accept for ourselves as a fact or truth of our being. But if you look at the whole idea of loneliness, you will find that it had to be first just that—an idea in your mind. If you keep that idea and re-inforce it—"I'm lonely," or "I don't have anybody," or "I have no friends"—then you begin to breathe life into that state of mind and eventually you will feel it subconsciously where your emotions are. This leads to feelings of rejection, alienation, and generally a sense that life has dealt you a rough blow.

Be Honest with Yourself

Before you can break the grip of loneliness, you have to work with your feelings about yourself. As long as you accept the idea of loneliness in your life, it will control and keep you in this frame of mind. Look at yourself as a person and ask yourself, "What has caused me to get in the state of consciousness to believe that there's nobody around but me? Why do I reject others? Why do I feel that others have rejected me and that I have no friends?" In other words, the first step is just being honest with yourself.

This was Jesus' message all the time. He was constantly teaching us how to look at ourselves and see what we are, what we need, what we have to do about a particular situation. That's still the biggest challenge we have today. We really don't take time to look at the situation we're in and to work with it honestly.

Recognize, then, that if you're going to think in terms of loneliness, then you are accepting it and really not participating in the beautiful life-stream around you. So the first step is to look at yourself and see what got you to the point of rejection, alienation, friendlessness. Facing the answers to these questions is the first step to ending loneliness. Psychologists have found that people who are lonely in their old age were lonely when they were younger. We sort of get into a box and accept loneliness, telling ourselves that there's nothing that can be done about it. But if you don't like the way your life is going, if you don't want it to be this way for years to come, then you must begin *now to* take responsibility for it.

Your Work Can Work for You

What is your occupation? Are you happy in it? Is it fulfilling? Do you really get excited about going to work? Some people get up and pray about getting through Monday. By Friday, they're happy because the weekend is coming. But then, here comes Monday again. What a vicious circle! On Fridays they're excited, the work week is over. Come Monday, they're falling apart again.

Reexamine your occupation. See what it means to you. Is it an excitement? Do you enjoy doing what you do? As you begin to move into areas of work that are enjoyable, you attract to you people who enjoy their work just as you do. That could be the beginning of a good, positive relationship.

Perhaps you're not working. Maybe you're retired or at home for some other reason. If so, look at the time of day that you feel most alone. Keep a diary of those times so that you can identify them. That's the very time of day when you should find a special place to be. This would be a good time to go out and do some volunteer work. We hear all the time of cutbacks taking place in employment situations. In many agencies, staff will be moving out because of economic reasons. But those agencies could still survive if people like you would go in and volunteer their time and talent.

Some people feel they don't have any talent. We all have talent. Maybe you haven't discovered yours yet, and that too could be a reason for your loneliness. The only way to discover your talent is to take some step toward seeking it. Being of service does wonders toward removing the attitude of loneliness, and until you begin to change this attitude, you can't draw to you those who might erase the sense of loneliness.

Learn to Be Other-Centered

People often don't realize that they give off an air of what they are. Some call these vibrations. When you are giving off a negative air, others pick it up and don't want to be around you because you are so self-concerned. Self-concern can be turned into a beautiful experience. It can lead you to wonderful discoveries about yourself. But don't take it so far that it gives others the idea that you "don't want to be bothered."

Living *Alone Doesn't Have to Mean* Being *Alone*

Another thing I want to suggest is that you work with your past beliefs and negative attitudes about what it means to live by yourself. A person without a partner is not less of a person. Whenever you find yourself complaining about being by yourself, that's the time to remember some of the beautiful scriptural references that can give you comfort, peace, a desire to do something about yourself or for someone else. The secret to overcoming loneliness is to associate yourself with something more comprehensive, to come in tune with that Spirit, that Presence that is within you waiting to be tapped.

Remember my comment about the people who live for

Friday? Well, at the other end of the spectrum are those who hate to see Friday come around because it signals being alone. I find this often with young women who live alone. When these women leave their jobs on Friday, everybody in the office seems to have plans for the weekend. These women may not have a thing in mind, but rather than admit this to their coworkers, they'll say they've got big weekends ahead. When they get back to the office Monday morning, they feel they have to say they've participated in certain activities because everyone else is talking about exciting weekends.

If you have no plans for the weekend, why does that have to be so terrible? It's all right. That may be your time to unfold your Christ self, to really find out what is going on inside of you and to get to know the beautiful Spirit inside you. Jesus said the first of all the commandments is "Thou shalt love the Lord thy God with all thy heart, and with all thy soul, and with all thy mind, and with all thy strength" (Mark 12:30); and the second is "Thou shalt love thy neighbor as thyself" (Mark 12:31). The first neighbor you have is the person inside you.

You have to look at where you are in your frame of reference with God as Spirit. In 1 John 4:4 we read: "Greater is He that is in you, than he that is in the world." "He" represents Spirit. So first of all, there is that about you which is so beautiful that it alone should tell you that you have no cause for loneliness. You have the Spirit of the living God abiding right within you. But the only way you're going to know it's there is to speak those words, to dwell on beautiful thoughts, and to really give yourself an opportunity to listen to the still, small voice within you, which is also a comforting voice.

The apostle Paul said that he had learned how to be content in whatever location he found himself. He learned how to be humble and how to abound. Likewise, it doesn't matter where you live—in a home with family, alone in an apartment, or a senior citizens' high-rise. If you will begin to touch your inner resource, you'll begin to find out that you really are not alone. Once you tap that inner resource, everything in the outer falls in place. You begin to have the order you need, the joy that you want.

Look to Yourself First

You can't go outside to cure loneliness. You have to go inside. And you have to recognize that there is a Presence as well as a Power within you. I have been alone physically and mentally many times in my life, but never alone spiritually. Whenever I feel depressed, I've always come back to something inspirational—a Scripture, a particular place I enjoy being, a book, a song, or listening to recordings of inspirational music. Once you put yourself in an inspirational frame of mind, your thoughts begin to move through the spiritual current, and a peace comes over you. Peace erases loneliness. Love erases loneliness. When you learn that you can love and appreciate yourself, you don't have time to be lonely. And as Jesus said in John 14: 15–18:

> If ye love me, keep my commandments. And I will pray the Father, and He shall give you another Comforter, that He may abide with you forever . . . ye know Him; for He dwelleth with you, and shall be in you.

Finally, let me caution that it will take time for you to overcome your loneliness-thinking pattern—but it *can* be overcome. Turn to the fourteenth chapter of John and read those comforting words. Know that you are unrepeatable, that you are a miracle, that you are a unique child of God, and that God in you makes the difference. Be reminded of the goodness of the Spirit in you, and know that you are not alone.

Regardless of whether or not there are any people around, you can know that God loves you and that God has not left you alone. That Presence and that power of Spirit in you is God. It will comfort you so that you will not have to have anybody else around. Accept that Truth, and you will eventually realize that you are always in the presence of the Lord.

AFFIRMATIONS

1. *God is always with me. I am never alone.*

2. *God is with me through every moment of the day or night.*

3. *There is no absence of God anywhere, so wherever I am God is.*

4. *God indwells me, surrounds me, enfolds me.*

5. *Right where I am in this experience I know the truth that God is with me.*

6. *There is nothing to fear, for God is and will protect me, guide me, and comfort me.*

7. *God is my constant companion. He protects me at night while I sleep. He is with me during the day.*

8. *I feel God's Presence and the light casts out all thoughts of fear and depression.*

9. *I am inspired, loved, and filled with courage.*

10. *I am one with God. I now remove from my mind any false belief about myself.*

11. *I am fully conscious of my true worth, and those I meet are conscious of it.*

12. *I know that somewhere in the universe there is someone who needs me as much as I need him/her and who will never be satisfied until I become a part of the completed circle. We need each other. Creative Intelligence knows where each of us is and is bringing us together. Our meeting will be the richest fulfillment of our lives. Each enjoys the other just as he or she is. I now release this desire to Creative Intelligence that has brought every happy, harmonious couple together, making them one. Thank You, Father, for answered prayer. And it is so!*

--- ✳ ---

CHAPTER NINE

After the Divorce

*W*e hear so much today about the high divorce rate in this country.

The National Center for Women and Retirement Research, in their publication *Women and Divorce: Turning Your Life Around*, stated that:

> The adjustment from a married to a single status is difficult for most people. The feelings of loneliness, anger, fear, anxiety, and insecurity are emotions that are commonly experienced by people going through a divorce. While these feelings are normal and a necessary part of your emotional adjustment, they make planning and decision making difficult. Some of the unique problems women face during this period are financial hardship, discrimination, child care, returning to the work force, and retaining a lawyer.

We generally use the word *divorce* to mean the dissolution of a marriage. In the broader sense of the word, however, we sometimes are divorced from *ourselves* because we really don't know our true selves. Sometimes people are emotionally divorced from their jobs, from their families, from their environment, just sort of functioning at a level of thinking that they don't need anything or anybody else. This causes them to separate themselves out.

But I want to look particularly at divorce as it relates to marriage, and I want to use the Bible reference Matthew 19:6, in which Jesus says, "*What therefore God hath joined together, let not man put asunder.*" In this particular chapter, Jesus was explaining to the people about their misuse of the bill of divorcement given to them during Moses' time. All it took then was for a man to say three times to his wife "I divorce you," and it was over. Jesus, then, was rebuking them for their attitude that they could just run away from situations rather than work through them.

At one time I seemed to have a lot of men coming to me for counseling about divorces. I remember one young man in particular who shared his experience with me. He had married and moved his wife here from another city; after having been here for six months, his wife was unhappy and didn't like the city. For any number of reasons she had decided that she didn't want to be married; she wanted a divorce, she wanted to go back to her family and to the city from which she came. This young man was in his early thirties, making a good living, traveling all over the world. He just couldn't understand how his marriage could be falling apart after such a short time. And to make it worse, he and his wife couldn't talk about the situation.

This wasn't his first marriage. Fresh out of high school, he had married his childhood sweetheart and thought it the zenith of his life. That marriage didn't last long, either—no more than a couple of years. Both partners explained the failure of that marriage by saying that they were too young. Now, at the age of thirty-three, he was facing his second divorce.

As I talked to this young man and began to understand what had led him into his two marriages, it occurred to me that we would all be so much better off if our peers, parents, friends, and acquaintances whom we respect would encourage premarital counseling, rather than routinely expecting everyone to get married. In our society there seems to be a bias that people who aren't married are strange animals. But with proper counseling, many people might find that for whatever reasons, they don't actually need to be married at all. Think how many divorces *that* would prevent!

What Are We Expecting from Marriage, Anyway?

Let me stop for a moment and share what I think is an excellent definition of marriage by Eric Butterworth, one of the most respected writers of inspirational books. "*Marriage is the license by which two people who have seen the greater possibilities in each other may work together to bring forth those possibilities.*" It is a laboratory of individual unfoldment. In a marriage, then, two people ought to be able to see beyond the image they project and see the good behind the image. They ought to see and accept each other as individuals who have come together to work at something worthwhile and to bring their good into a happy, loving union.

By contrast, we ministers too often feel that when we conduct a wedding ceremony, it seals the marriage. But the ceremony does not seal the *attitude,* it does not seal the *consciousness* that two people must have when they join in marriage. For the marriage to be successful, the couple must bring to it an attitude of working together toward understanding and supporting each other, not just a casual, "Well, we're married now, so we must be in love!"

And this suggests two other problems that often keep marriages from being successful: the misunderstanding of the word *love,* and the idea that someone can *make us* happy. As for our misinterpretation of the word *love,* what we need to understand is that one can't just marry and expect the mate to provide love automatically. The love has to flow *within* each of us; it must be activated internally, so to speak, before it can be felt. And as for the idea of others bringing us happiness, about all that another person can really do is help you enjoy what happiness you already possess. You've got to know before you get married that you can be happy with yourself. Then when you meet someone else who also knows this self-happiness, the two of you come together and your happiness is reflected in each of you. In other words, love *comes from* you; love meets love in another individual; love binds itself to more love and becomes a beautiful experience.

You Must Take Responsibility for Yourself

To the young man who had come to me seeking counseling, I said, "All right, so here you are with two marriages that ended in divorce. What are you doing about *yourself* now? Have you really stopped and looked at yourself to see if you feel good about yourself? You may be seeking happiness from someone else or from some outside object, when what you need to do is learn to build some happiness within you."

What am I talking about? *Self-esteem.* This simply means what we think or feel about ourselves, what kinds of attitudes we have built up over a period of years based on what others say, what others have told us about ourselves and how they have encouraged us to think about ourselves. Many "bad" marriages result when one party or the other is lacking self-esteem and therefore seeking to ease the pain and reach a desired psychological level by relying on someone else. This doesn't work.

I told this to my counselee and said that before he made another step, he had to begin working with himself. First, he had to reconnect himself with his spiritual self. He answered that besides going to his own weddings, he really hadn't been to church. "But more than going to church," I said, "how do you feel about your love of God? About just knowing that there's something greater within you that you can hold on to, that you can know will be there?"

The Scriptures, after all, tell us that there is a Spirit in us and that the inspiration of that Spirit gives us understanding. The extent to which we stir up that Spirit is an expression of the way we feel about ourselves.

I assured the young man that I wasn't blaming him for the divorce—there are always two sides, and some people say three sides. The important thing to remember, though, is that divorce is not the end. From there, you can begin to work with yourself, to pick up the pieces. Every day you get up, seek that inner guidance, direction, and you will begin to know that you are a person, that no person and no thing can keep your good from you.

Remember, life is filled with change, and every time you go through a change, it's part of your own personal growth and development. We go from classroom to classroom. Each experience you have can strengthen you if you will see it as an opportunity to look at how well you're functioning. As I said, one can be divorced from anything—including God. Some of us don't even know that we are perfect, whole children of God. We just kind of move through the universe at our own rate of speed, and suddenly it takes an experience like a divorce to help us see what we ought to be about. So if you've recently gone through a divorce, don't throw up your hands, don't get angry, don't hold hate or resentment, don't try for the "payback." But stop and realize that this experience has come into your life for your soul growth. You drew this experience to yourself because you drew a particular person into your life.

Maybe you ran too fast. Maybe you didn't even try to discuss what you ought to have done about it. Maybe you didn't go for counseling; maybe you didn't seek the Lord; maybe you didn't seek guidance. If that's the way it was, then accept it and say, "It's all right." Then ask yourself: "Where do I go from here? How do I pick up the pieces and begin getting myself in divine order so I can live to the fullest, so I can know that after the divorce I can still be a total person?" Here are some steps that may help you:

1. Reconnect yourself with your Divine Source. Recognize that there is a Spirit in you, that God has helped you to get through the pain and the hurt. Just say the Lord's Prayer and you will know that you don't have to hold any animosity or thoughts of getting even. When you learn to release a person to his or her own highest good, then you can stand on your own two feet and be what you ought to be; you can know that person is no longer a part of your life. In other words, in releasing you can begin moving to your own highest good.

Jesus said, "What *God* hath joined together," but the problem is that many times God has not been in the midst of our marital situation, because we're just functioning at a human level. But if you now find yourself in a divorce experience, first of all recognize that there is a Presence, there is a Power—God the Good, omnipotent—that you can turn to and ask for guidance. As I said to the counselee, go back and look at your faith and trust. See what you can build on. Let's not forget that no matter how successful we are in our careers and other outer endeavors, it's God within us that helps us to be the successes we are. Before you touch a light switch, the electricity is there, but until you turn the switch on, you'll never have the light. So it is with the ever-present God.

Further, as you reconnect with God through your moments of quiet meditation and reflection—"Be still and know that I am God" (Psalms 46:10)—you give yourself a greater opportunity to enter into new visions of yourself. You begin to know and feel your spirituality. Then the concept of Spirit, mind, and body is no longer missing in your spiritual understanding. Some of us will discover our spirituality from practicing the stillness without benefit of a group experience. Others of us may need the religious organization through which the rituals, celebrations, classes, and support groups begin to draw us into a deeper awareness of our relationship to God. Many persons are choosing nontraditional paths of religion and finding the answers and support they desire. When I became one of the divorce statistics, I found peace with a nontraditional group from which I followed my lifelong dream of entering into the ministry. I had been a member of a Baptist church from my childhood, but I found when I became a divorcée, I didn't fit anymore as far as the traditional groups were concerned. I found in the new group an opportunity to discover me, to connect with God in a way I had never experienced before. I slowly released guilt—the guilt that God would not forgive me for repeating vows that said "till death do us part." Coming home to God gives you peace in knowing that so-called mistakes can only help you in your spiritual growth and development. You get up, dust yourself off, and keep moving!

2. Forgive your former mate as you forgive yourself.
It makes no sense to harbor feelings of guilt, resentment, or

bitterness at a time like this. The legal and physical details of breaking up a household, and the emotional trauma, are enough to deal with. Why add unnecessary hard feelings to the burden?

You don't know what will come from the experience, but at least give yourself a forgiveness treatment. If you don't forgive, all the anger and resentment will affect you, because whatever you're feeling toward someone else affects you first. In affecting you, it affects your job, your relationships with other people, and every aspect of your life.

When we forgive ourselves, we free our minds from unpleasant memories, thus giving us a fresh outlook on life. Forgiveness of ourselves and others is vital to our peace of mind and the health of our bodies. We now know medically how emotions of anger and hate affect the immune system and cause diseases.

It is also important that we not condemn ourselves for making decisions that were best for that time in our lives. If we hold on to failures and injustices of the past, it affects our success in the present and the future. I attended a family week program recently and heard this poem:

> As children bring their broken toys
>> with tears for us to mend,
> I brought my broken dreams to God,
>> because He is my friend.
> But then,
>> instead of leaving Him
>> in peace to work alone,
> I hung around and tried to help,
>> with ways that were my own.
> At last I snatched them back and cried,
> "How can you be so slow?"

"My child," He said, "what could I do?
You never did let go!" (Author unknown)

Let Go. Let God!

3. Remind yourself that there is a lesson in this for your good. Then thank God for the opportunity to learn the lesson. Regardless of what happens in any life experience, you can pick up the pieces, mend them with the help of God, and keep moving. You need not stop. God in you will carry you through any situation. Keep in mind there is a personal growth through involvement. To help yourself become an active single person, try some of these suggestions:

1. Become active in your community through volunteer service.
2. Take up activities where you can meet others with similar needs and interests.
3. Get involved in or start support groups for families of patients with life-threatening illnesses.
4. Pursue the dream you've kept locked up inside.
5. Develop relationships with new friends.
6. Take a class, join a club or group of some kind.

I spoke on the phone one day with a divorced young man who acted on the still, small voice within and moved from the state of California to Denver, Colorado. He told me he had just left a dance class. My response was, "How wonderful!" He said, "Well, I've just moved here and I want to make new friends, so I decided what better way than to join a dance group!"

God Yesterday, God Today, God Tomorrow

Once you begin to love yourself again and the God within, you will attract a person who also is experiencing that same love of God. Then you can begin a new relationship, work at it, and know that you can see it through. If that person does not come into your experience, don't worry about it. Just involve yourself in your church, involve yourself in various activities, in volunteer work perhaps—whatever will help you build a positive mental attitude and be the child of God you were meant to be. And if the right person *does* come along and you choose not to marry again, that's all right too.

Affirm for yourself: *Changes may come in my life, but God in me is the yesterday, today, and tomorrow.* No matter what it is, no matter what you're going through, you don't have to feel sorry for yourself. Instead, direct your attention to the Presence within you; speak words that will build up rather than tear down; release the other person and know that in releasing, you gain your own sense of stability. Continue to put the light of God around yourself and the situation.

Yes, divorce can be painful. But if you'll just touch that Spirit in you, you'll find that God allows us to make a comeback even from our most painful mistakes. Just be happy and mindful that the God in you is a God of love and peace. We are always under grace through Christ Jesus, so hold on just a little longer.

AFFIRMATIONS

1. *I accept my divorce as a decision I reached at the time of my challenge in marriage.*
2. *God loves me always.*
3. *I face each new day knowing through the Christ in me, I can face any difficulty.*
4. *Create in me a clean heart, O God; and renew a right spirit within me (Psalms 51:10).*
5. *Be still and know that I am God (Psalms 46:7).*
6. *Peace be still in me and through me.*
7. *Only good can come from this experience.*
8. *I now release worn-out relationships and conditions.*
9. *As I release things of the past, I am also being released and guided into the present and future.*
10. *The forgiving love of Jesus Christ frees me from mistakes of the past, present, and future.*

CHAPTER TEN

✳

Born to Be Rich

*I*n the recent past we seem to have been surrounded by a national consciousness that insisted there wasn't enough of anything to go around, that there would be nothing for future generations but suffering and preparation for war. So much of this negative emotion found its way into the universe that I reassured everyone, as I reassured myself, that a loving Father-Mother God would not deny goodness when the children came back, as did the prodigal son. To begin with, we must learn to listen to the inner guidance, the intuition, the still, small voice of God in whatever we do, whether it's in our church, in our homes, in our offices, or in our work sites.

But today, history is repeating itself. We're talking about inflation, the ecology, a growth in population. I've been speaking at colleges and high schools, and I pick up a fearful attitude on the part of students who are unsure of what their future holds in the face of proposed federal cutbacks in educational funds. They're afraid that they will not have an opportunity to make it through school because doors will be closed to them.

Even so, when I answer the question "Is wealth for a select few?" I have to say, "No!" The problem is simply that we have gotten so caught up in the physical aspects of living that we've forgotten that there is another dimension waiting for us to use in all its power and glory to move into our lives the goodness we were created to have. We were created out of love. We were created to have the goodness of our Creator. And the Scriptures tell us that the Father knows what we have need of even before we ask.

The question then becomes, Who are we asking? Who are we looking to for our financial needs? Who are we seeing as the source? I believe with all my heart, soul, and mind that there is only one source, and that's God. I believe that God as Spirit, as an Infinite Intelligence, works with us through our conscious thinking. Remember, whatever we are conscious of is what we experience in our daily lives.

We think and act and feel based on what our human intelligence tells us. But we must also be bathed with the Spirit of God; and this means we must know how to speak and think Truth. There are many instances in the Scriptures where men and women were "up against the wall" so to speak, and knew of no way out. But they always seemed to find their way back to that other dimension, that spiritual self, and to recognize that they could do nothing of themselves, but with God, all things were possible to them.

I love the words Jesus spoke in Matthew, the sixth chapter, verses thirty through thirty-four:

> Wherefore, if God so clothe the grass of the field, which today is, and tomorrow is cast into the oven, shall He not much more clothe you, O ye of little faith?
> Therefore take no thought, saying, What shall

we eat? or, What shall we drink? or, Wherewithal shall we be clothed?

(For after all these things do the Gentiles seek:) for your heavenly Father knoweth that ye have need of all these things.

But seek ye first the kingdom of God, and His righteousness; and all these things shall be added unto you.

Take therefore no thought for the morrow; for the morrow shall take thought for the things of itself. Sufficient unto the day is the evil thereof.

I believe that wherever you are today in your awareness of how your financial needs can be met, it has to do with childhood influences. Some of us came from an environment in which we had plenty. Others came out of environments where all we had was anger and resentment and envy and criticism and lack.

So many of us have come from backgrounds that we label negatively. And when we label people, they take those labels and come to believe very strongly that they can't be anything but what they've been labeled. That's where the breakthrough has to come—to help a person know that it is not the label but one's attitude that counts. You must have faith to believe that no matter what the conditions are, if you can keep yourself in tune with Spirit and believe that a way will be made, then *it will be so.*

I, for instance, came out of an environment that might be labeled a "poor" one. But I was raised by my grandmother, who knew that there was something beyond the human. She always looked to that spiritual self for guidance and direction. I remember times when my grandmother would cut out pasteboard and put it in my shoes when they were worn thin and she didn't have the money to have them half-soled. What she was doing was taking what she had and using it. That idea had to come from someplace. Deep within her, she wanted me to go to school. She did not want my feet to touch the ground, yet she had no money. So God, that Infinite Intelligence, worked through her mind and gave her the idea; and therefore I never had to miss a day of school.

And throughout the years of my upbringing by my grandmother, in the words that she spoke to me I never heard the word *poor*. And things were meager there. I can remember a potbellied stove and having to "split a chunk," as we called it, and breaking up kindling to make a fire for that stove. Nevertheless, I was taught to be thankful and to know that if I thanked God for what I was receiving, more would come.

Now from that very modest beginning to this present time, I have seen God's spiritual laws work. I know what it means to work your way through school. I worked my way through as a bus girl, dishwasher, and maid—not what one would consider "status" positions. But in everything, I learned to be thankful for the opportunity to grow spiritually, mentally, and emotionally.

I wish I had kept a diary or journal of every door that opened for me when I had thought there was no way. I wish I had written down the exact feelings I had when a door opened for me during my second year at Texas Southern University, when I had no tuition money the day school began and somebody let me register anyhow! God always works through some channel to open a door. But it is your conscious awareness, it is your belief, your thought that you use to connect yourself to this power called God.

Labels! Just as I'd never heard the word *ghetto* until I got to graduate school, didn't know a thing about it, you have to rise above labels in your thinking. Look at them and decide that you can survive and rise above them. And always keep your focus on the Lord.

Use Your Inner Resources

The first thing you have to be aware of is that there is a Presence and a Power that works through you when you allow It to. We have to learn that what we are looking for is right inside us. If we just listen, we'll find that we have so much to work with. You can start in a one-room apartment; you can start in a five-room house. But wherever you are, look around you and begin to see what's there for you to use. To become fully aware of our capacity for prosperity, we need to retrain our thinking. We need to look at our beginnings only long enough to recognize that no matter what we have come through, it's okay. When you recognize that you can use past experiences as though they were stones across a creek, then you realize it doesn't matter what your background is, because those experiences will act as stepping stones for you.

How can we open ourselves through the retraining of our minds and come to understand that prosperity is ours? There's a perfectly logical process involved.

1. You have to know that you don't depend on other persons or conditions for your prosperity. You bless persons, you bless conditions as channels, but God is the source of your supply. God provides His own amazing channels of supply to you right now. But if you depend on the boss, if you depend on the paycheck—suppose the paycheck doesn't come? Then what do you do? There has to be another channel. You have to learn not to give up if one door closes, not to throw up your hands. Instead, seek another idea from God, wait for it to come, and then move on it.

2. You have to let go of worn-out ideas, worn-out conditions, worn-out relationships. Sometimes we get caught up with ideas and conditions. Inflation is one such idea.

You have to release that kind of thinking from your mind and move away from relationships and people who reinforce it. Move away from people who constantly say that there is no answer, no hope and no future for someone like you. Refuse to accept worn-out labels. Release them.

3. The act of release is magnetic. Through releasing, you draw to you that which is yours. Let go and grow! Let go of the negative thinking. Let go of the impossibility thoughts that say there's no solution, and watch as you are flooded with hope.

4. You must forgive all that has offended you, within and without. Things past, things present, things future, you must forgive. You must forgive everything and everybody who could *possibly* need forgiveness. No matter how badly you've been hurt, you will not grow spiritually if you don't forgive.

Sometimes we are blocked from receiving our good because we have so much anger. We're resentful of our supervisor; we're resentful of people we work with; we're resentful of our former mates. You have to stop that kind of thinking and realize that in forgiving yourself, you open up a flow of ideas that will lead you to know what to do. Forgiveness is an inner act. It's releasing a negative emotion about somebody or something. Many think that they can't get a raise on their job or fear that they're going to be laid off. You have got to forgive that whole situation and know that if that door closes, then certainly you have a gift from God, a talent that you can use elsewhere. And when you realize that fact, you can stop looking to use your gift in the same place you just left. You see, it doesn't matter. You can start where you are; you can learn to use what you have.

5. Do the work you love, and love the work you do. When you love something, it draws to you more opportunities to express yourself in the area that brings you pleasure. As your pleasure grows, so does your opportunity for prosperity. As your channels of love open, you are able to relate more freely to those around you and, eventually, you will find more and more opportunity coming your way, from many sources and resources.

Wealth Is for YOU

Wealth is *not* for a select few, because wealth means "well-being." Whether it's wealth of mind, wealth of health, wealth of material goods—no matter what the goodness that you desire, know that God did not design this world so there would always be the haves and the have-nots. *Man* has structured that. But those of us who believe must use our spiritual self and stand on the promises of God and know that doors will open for us. Know where you want to go. Make the decision to have whatever it is you desire from life, then act on that decision.

Don't give up; set your goals and picture what it is you need to do to achieve them. See yourself making it step by step.

Most of all, remember that your heavenly Father knows what you have need of before you ask. Learn to still your anxious thoughts. Look at the flowers. Even with the changing of the seasons, they have a natural flow. And if you will just learn to move with that same flow, the flow of God, you will know that your good is at hand. Take your mind off your anxieties for a few moments and just say the following affirmations:

AFFIRMATIONS

1. *God, I'm Yours. You created me out of Yourself, and I believe that Your will for me is all good. Wherever my financial need may be expressing itself, I know that with You all things are possible. I thank You right now for every channel, every door that opens. I'm coming back to You, knowing that You will cleanse and feed my mind and bathe me in Your Spirit until I know that there's an answer, there's an answer, there's an answer. And I accept that answer right now. Through the Christ within, thank You, Father; thank You, Father; thank You, Father. And So It Is!*

2. *My Heavenly Father's good is always available to me.*

3. *There is no absence of God anywhere.*

4. *The infinite thinker thinks through me.*

5. *The majesty of the Almighty, the unlimited Good, are demonstrated through me.*

6. *I have faith in God as my unfailing, all-providing Source.*

7. *I am a spiritual being and all that I need flows to me unimpeded, marked with my name, addressed to me.*

8. *No one can take my good from me for it is mine by right of consciousness.*

9. *My Heavenly Father knows what I need and supplies it without delay.*

10. *In Christ I am unfettered, unbound, triumphant, glorious, splendid, free!*

11. *Nothing can bind or limit me. Thanks, God. And so it is!*

CHAPTER ELEVEN

✳

Your Ticket to Health

For just a few moments, allow yourself to think about the word *ticket*.

As you think about that word, does it occur to you that we are living in an age when we seem to need a ticket for everything we do? Whatever we participate in, wherever we go, we have to have some kind of ticket. It may be a ticket for parking, for a sporting event, or for a trip by plane or train. There is always some form of card, some kind of slip, something that we use to indicate that we should be admitted or served.

Tickets, then, prove that we are entitled to whatever it is we are trying to access. In that case, why not a *ticket* to health? And if you can accept the idea of a ticket to health, take it one step further and accept these words: *I am my own ticket to health.*

So often we mistakenly believe that what happens outside of us has nothing to do with the way we think and the way we feel. When we have purchased a ticket, for instance, and something happens to displease us, we might blame the thing for which we purchased the ticket. For example, you take time from your busy schedule to go to a sporting event, but the home team plays so badly that you get angry at them. After the game, you look at your ticket and throw it away or tear it up in disgust.

Or you're taking a business trip and you have to catch two planes to get to your destination. The first plane is delayed at the gate and this causes you to miss your connecting flight. As you sit in an airport in a distant city, waiting for the next flight to your destination, you look at your ticket and think, "I knew I should have taken the other airline! This one is always late!"

Having fixed the blame, then you allow yourself to indulge in a bad mood because you have been inconvenienced by, or displeased with, what the ticket led you to. But think a little deeper about the situation. If you are your own ticket, then the ticket represents your *own conscious thought*. And if you are in a bad mood because of something the ticket admitted you to, then your thoughts just represent what you think about *what you are* and *what you do*. If that's the case, you can change your attitude about what the ticket led you to and instantly put an end to your bad mood.

Here's a Ticket You Can Fix

In the first example, if the team played poorly and you have just spent an afternoon watching a one-sided game that put you in a bad mood, then it is your *attitude* about how you spent your time that has put you in a bad mood. In the second example, if you missed a connecting flight because your original flight was delayed, then you are in a bad mood because you perceive that by missing your connecting flight you are not in your right place at the right time. And whether you realize it or not, both re-actions are affecting your health. So think for a moment, "How can I be my own ticket to health?"

Realize first that health means *wholeness*. It means the integration of Spirit in our physical being, in our mental being, and in our emotional being. How, then, can you be your own ticket to health? How can you bring about wholeness through using what you already have? The answer is that by your divine inheritance you are fully "clothed"—you are the answer to your own needs. **Recognize that you are the answer to your own desires.**

Put God First

Coming out of the teachings of Jesus, I do believe Jesus is the greatest example of what man is to be in expression. I also believe that we learn from all religions. Of a truth, I know that we all teach love. Of a truth, I know that we all believe in the brotherhood of man. I also know the principle of loving God with all my heart, with all my soul, and with all my mind. I recognize too that not all of us call this Intelligence, this Presence, *God*. However I want you to know, wherever you are right now with whatever you call that Presence, that it does not matter to me. I have to call It what I like to call It because It has meaning for me. So I call it *God*.

Having said that, let me say that if you are going to be the ticket to your own health, you want to be the doer of your own wholeness. This means that you have to know and express that you truly are made in the image and likeness of God. If you are going to experience yourself as perfect and whole, your first step must be to always take God as your priority. We have a lot of priorities in our lives. We have a lot of things that we put first. But I want to suggest that you **let God, let the Essence, let the very Spirit of your being be your first priority.** Always. Remember the first commandment God gave to Moses was,

"You shall have no other gods before me" (Exodus 20:3).

When I was a social worker, I often found that when things were going rough, when things appeared to be too challenging, the best thing I could do was just to close my office door, get still, and acknowledge that *God is all there is; there is nothing else.* I just stood firm on that affirmation until I could pull myself together and know that what I was looking at was a way of reaching myself. When I acknowledged that God was my priority, I knew that I could make it through.

Making the Contact

Scripture advises us, "In all your ways acknowledge Him, and He will make straight your paths" (Proverbs 3:6). When you choose God as your priority, then you know that you make no step until you first have that time of quietness, that time when you choose to seek, to know, to acknowledge who and what you are, that time you take to "regroup," to be identified with the Oneness, the perfection that you are.

Nothing else should come before your making contact with the Spirit of Truth that is within you. Recognize that when you go to your Inner Spirit, you will always know what to do. **By going first to your Inner Spirit, you will always know what decisions to make and how to carry them out.**

So it is important to recognize that when you see God first in everything, when you seek the answers through that first priority, then all things work together for your good because you do love God, because you do put God first in your life. That's not a challenge for any of us, because any time that we choose to stop and be still and remember who and what we are, then we know who our priority is. So that's the first step in being your own ticket to health: **Make God your first priority.**

Learn to Listen

We listen through prayer and meditation. Prayer is that time you use to talk and express your needs to God. Meditation, on the other hand, is that time when you listen for that inner guidance, for that inner voice that tells you just what it is you are to do. *Listening is so important.* So often we find ourselves talking constantly about what should be, what could be done if only we had this or that. But too often we don't take the time to follow up the prayer with a time of listening so the still, small voice within us can be heard.

At one point when I was traveling quite a bit and was very weary, I got a telephone call from my mother in Los Angeles. She said, "You were on my mind so strongly that I had to call. I didn't know what was going on, but I just felt the urge to call you. You know you always tell me, 'Mother, follow your first mind.' " Her call that day was exactly what I needed. I'm so thankful that she listened to that still, small voice.

An important thing to understand about prayer is that the words we speak in prayer must not be about changing God. Those words are to change *us,* to lift us up until we know that we don't have to be concerned once we have prayed our prayer. **Our job is to listen for the still, small voice.** Sometimes it comes just as peace over your soul. But somehow you *know* by that stillness that everything is working out by divine timing.

Follow Through

After we have prayed and after we have listened, we are told what to do. So many times when we get our answer of what to do, we fail to follow through. We do all kinds of things to avoid the work of following through. We talk back to ourselves:

"No, that can't be right!" or "Maybe it won't work." We even seek someone else's advice before we obediently follow through. This is the time, however, when we must take action, because if we do not, then we have not taken to heart what we have heard in the stillness. We have not believed that what we have been told can actually be so.

A classic example of following through comes to us in the story of Jesus' healing of a blind man. The Scriptures tell us:

> And they came to Bethsaida. And some people brought to Him a blind man, and begged Him to touch him. And He took the blind man by the hand, and led him out of the village; and when He had spit on his eyes and laid His hands upon him, He asked him, "Do you see anything?" And he looked up and said, "I see men; but they look like trees, walking." Then again He laid His hands upon his eyes; and he looked intently and was restored, and saw everything clearly (Mark 8:22–25).

You may be able to imagine the man's shock to have his sight restored after blindness. Just think how it must have been to have seen nothing for years and suddenly to see a blur of motion. But back up to the point where the man said what he saw looked like walking trees. Suppose Jesus had responded to this by shrugging His shoulders and saying, "Oh, well, I tried." Or take the part where Jesus attempted to lay His hands on the man's eyes again. Suppose at this point the man had said, "Oh, never mind! This is good enough."

Do you begin to understand the importance of following through? Jesus touched the blind man more than once before the healing was fulfilled because He knew that the healing, the wholeness, was there in its fullness. If it wasn't, there would have been no change at all in the man's condition. But Jesus knew that on the other side of the problem was the answer. Think of your own health problems in just this same way.

Like this man whose sight was restored in stages, we sometimes receive a shock when something looks like it is going to be a breakthrough in a condition, because we are so used to having the pain or the problem. We have lived with it from day to day, and when we first start moving toward God and wholeness, the least little bit of breakthrough sometimes is just shocking. We can learn from this two-part healing that **if we are working on something and we see just a tiny breakthrough, we must be thankful and keep on.**

Act on Your Strengths

There is another way to look at this business of following through, and that is to follow through with the use of our gifts and strengths. For example, how many times have you had revealed to you deep within the inner recesses of your soul what your strength is? Even after such a revelation, do you sometimes back off instead of taking action based on those strengths or gifts? If so, perhaps what you are lacking at such times is faith, the assurance that *what you are seeking already is.* In his boyhood, King David provided the perfect example of having the faith to follow through.

At the time I am speaking of, David tended his father's sheep while also serving as King Saul's armor bearer. But the Lord had already anointed him King over Israel. After David had been in the service of Saul for a while, the Philistines gathered their armies for battle and sent Goliath the giant to challenge the Israelites. For forty days the war went on, with no one having the courage to accept Goliath's challenge.

One day, David's father sent him with food for his brothers

who were at the battle site. While David's brothers were filling him in on the progress of the war, Goliath came out and issued his challenge. Everyone fled from Goliath, but David was offended. "Who is this uncircumcised Philistine, that he should defy the armies of the living God?" he asked (1 Samuel 17:26).

Word of David's defiance reached Saul, and the king sent for him. Let me go against Goliath, David told Saul. Saul tried to convince David that, as a youth, he was no match for the seasoned warrior Goliath. David said that he had defended his father's sheep against lions and bears and that he knew he could defend Israel against Goliath. You know the rest of the story. If you want to read it again, you'll find it in the First Book of Samuel, Chapter 17.

What was it that made David go against the seemingly undefeatable Goliath? Three factors gave David the courage to make his stand: 1. putting God first; 2. believing in what had been revealed to him to be his strength; and 3. *following up* on that strength. By taking these steps, you too can defeat the Goliaths in your life, the wreckers of your health and well-being.

Develop the Habit of Studying

When we attend conferences, revivals, or similar spiritual gatherings, we are infused with the spirit of the occasion and of the time. We buy books and we all share with our various teachers and the people in the audience who have had our experience of being uplifted. The excitement, the joy, the peace that we feel—can we go back to our homes, cities, towns, states and realize that what we have taken into our very being at those gatherings is still usable at home? Can we go back home and work the principles? Can we live the Truths that we have heard from the speakers from morning until night? Or is the gathering just a time of rejoicing and happiness that ends with the last Amen?

Why not go back and *"study"* to continue with what we have learned? It will be as good to us tomorrow as it was on the day we first received it, if we are willing to bring those uplifting moments back to life by studying on our own. One good way is to take the time to read something inspirational every day. We must be willing to take the time to have just a moment of quietness and to keep in mind that quietness and inspirational study contribute to our spiritual health.

It is important that we continue in our study, because by doing so we steal a moment of stillness from the hustle and bustle of everyday life. In these moments of stillness, of study, we reaffirm that we are children of God and that we have within us the ability to maintain our health of mind, body, and spirit.

Are You "Studied Up"?

At Hillside, we speak of being "prayed up"—that is, of having prayed sufficiently to meet the challenges of the day. We might also say that we can strive to be "studied up." We can immerse ourselves in Truth studies so that they sink into our beings. Then no matter what is happening, Truth will come up from the subconscious and it will remind us that all is well.

All *is* well. You *will* see it through. Your life is beautiful. No matter what seems to be going wrong, through prayer and the time of talking with the Father within, you will know that you are going to see it through. So study to show yourself approved by you. Study to understand.

Study to know that within you is all the knowledge you will ever need. At one time or another, we all had to start from scratch. Some of us may have started with an author whose books spoke to our particular needs. Others of us may have started with a Truth teacher, a preacher. Soon we began to realize that "I can move with this. I can do it on my own. I can work with it by myself." This is when we reap the joys of studying.

How Study Helped Restore Me

I remember a time in my life when I was facing a very serious physical challenge. I didn't realize that I was my own ticket to health, and so I relied entirely on the doctors. Whatever they said, whatever was done to me, it was fine. Finally some missionaries, who were not so-called New Thought people, came through the ward where I was. During their visit, they left some outdated copies of the monthly Unity publication, *Daily Word*.

How precious it was to me to pick up a *Daily Word* that was two years old and just read it. It was my first experience with Truth. As I read through the booklet, I came across a page that said readers could write to "Silent Unity." When I wrote, they sent me the "Prayer of Faith." The instructions that came with the prayer said to use it three times daily, to learn it if desired, but in any case to repeat it three times each day. I remember that when I came to the third verse of the prayer, I didn't want to say the first line, "God is my health; I can't be sick." It was difficult for me to say those words, when all around me were appearances not only of sickness, but of sickness unto death.

Nevertheless, I finally overcame my reluctance and said the line. Later I added the words, "In the name and through the power that is in the name of Jesus, the Christ, thank You, Father. Thank You, Father. Thank You, Father." I repeated the "Prayer of Faith" over and over every time a fear thought entered my mind. Each time my mind was invaded by the thought of never getting back home, never getting back to school, never seeing my family again, I'd go back to the very first line and say all the verses.

Each time I said those words, I felt a lifting up. There was something in me that I can't explain even to this day. I can never really put into words what happens to me at such times. But as a result of my experience, I know that when you take time to study, to find those words that appeal to the soul, and you repeat them over and over and over again, finally you realize that all is well, that you are the answer. **No matter what anybody tries to give you or do for you, it is up to you to be the answer to your own needs, to be the ticket to your own health.**

Claim Your Inheritance

After the prayer, the listening, the follow-through, and the study, you will realize beyond the shadow of a doubt that you *can claim all of your inheritance.* This too is part of your ticket to health, because your inheritance is all good—everywhere, evenly present. At any given time, your inheritance may be just a "thank you." Your inheritance may be just someone remembering to give you some small token of love. Whatever it is, *your inheritance is all of the good that comes your way;* and it makes you *feel* good, which, as we know, is a basic component of health.

You don't have to wait for something big to magnify. You can start with the little things that happen. It could be someone holding an elevator door; someone saying good morning; someone saying to you, "Gosh, you look great today!" It may be just an extra roll on the dinner plate.

Your inheritance is all of the good. You can start realizing that you should not take anything for granted. Your inheritance expresses itself in so many wonderful and beautiful ways because you are an heir of God and a joint heir with Christ Jesus. In that consciousness of knowing that all good is for you, you can **make the decision not to see bad, not to accept the things that appear to be bad, but to know that God's will for you is all good.**

Ask Yourself Why

If you are not experiencing that good, then you need to ask yourself why. You don't need to buy anything to find the answer to this question. You don't need to ask anybody else why. Just ask yourself, "What am I thinking? What have I accepted for myself? How have I altered my ticket to health?"

This self-questioning is important. The object of it is to realize that you do not necessarily have to maintain the same belief system with which you grew up. You do not have to maintain the same old ideas. Instead, you can truly look forward and understand that your inheritance says your good is everywhere, evenly present. Learn how to appreciate your good. Learn how to be thankful. **Learn how to not take anything for granted.**

If we are not careful, we will get to a point of not realizing that we must make moments to be thankful. We must take those moments to remind ourselves that we are children of God. There is nothing, not anything, that the Father will withhold from us if we are open and if we are receptive.

Know You Are That You Are

After you claim your inheritance, stand tall. Say to yourself, "I am that I am." Know that your spiritual growth is continuous. We are all in a state of *becoming*. Of a truth, though, you can say that you will be the very essence, the very spirit, the very totality, the very all-ness, the very intelligence of God that you are. Nobody can put you down. Nobody can say who you are, for you *are that you are.*

Think about this for a moment. Every time you speak the words *I am,* you are speaking your God name. All the words you put with *I am* are indicators of what you want to bring forth into your life. So when you speak the words *I am,* the question is: *What words do you attach to your "I am"?* Are you willing to stand up and say, "I'm so glad I am that I am, because I can hold the idea and know I can look beyond appearances to recognize that I am a child of God"? Or do you continually say, "I am sick," until that becomes the most insidious statement about you?

In my growing up and in my experience as a young woman, I was very outgoing. Whenever I am asked to speak and my resume is shared, I feel very humble to realize that I have come this far, although I am still under construction, I'm still growing and expanding. For a long time though, as outgoing as I was, as involved as I was, there was still that inside of me which ached. When I reached six feet five inches, I questioned, "God, why do I have to be so tall? Why is it that I tower over everybody else?" I really questioned! I really wanted to know! It was not until I came into the New Thought movement that I learned I was not a victim of my circumstances, but that I was really a victor. I came to know that if I learned to appreciate me, to accept me as I am and to take what I have and use it to the best of my ability, that would be my first step in realizing that people would love me as I am.

"Caretakers of the Caretaker"

Now, maybe you have not had an experience such as this. Nevertheless, I meet people all the time who are smiling on the outside and really hurting on the inside. Sometimes we are so concerned about the outer—the color of our hair, the shape of our eyes, the shape of our bodies. We go through so many changes about our physical selves that we forget that we are more than human. The fact is that there is an essence inside us that is the basis of our being. Our body temples are simply the caretakers of that inner Spirit. But we are the caretakers of the caretaker. *We are the ticket to our own health.*

How well do you perform your caretaking function? We in this country are so geared to physical movement. We take great joy in saying, "Oh, my life is just so hectic!" Unless we are just busy, busy, busy, we think we are not justifying our existence. I know your body has complained from time to time, *Rest!* and you didn't rest. It has asked you from time to time to *Take a few moments to be still!* Did you do it?

Only You Can Do It

You are not just passing through the universe by chance. *You are here to do something that only you can do.* If you are the person who walks into an office and becomes the peacemaker by a smile or by your quietness, that's a great thing to do and be. But you cannot do it if you haven't taken care of your own physical, mental, and spiritual health. When you begin to realize how beautiful you are and how important you are to the universe, then you will know how important it is that you make good use of that ticket you hold. No one else is going to do this for you; no one else *can* do it for you.

Yes, you are your own ticket. You are your way to being the wholeness that you can be. You can make the decision to be whole in body, in mind, in spirit and emotions; or you can make the decision not to be. Since you know how life evolves and since you have heard speaker after speaker say this same thing to you over and over, you must know by now that the choice rests with you. Even though you may know yourself to be a "born winner," the choice to win still rests with you. You can make whatever change is necessary in your life, in your world, in your affairs.

As you realize that *your ticket is your own conscious thought,* you will understand that when you think, and when you put your feeling nature into what you think, you will bring forth your own wholeness. Sometimes we get off the track, though. Sometimes we forget who we are. But by the grace of God, we have the blessed opportunity to come back on track, to put ourselves back into alignment by the conscious choice of thought and word. We can reverse any "off-track" thought simply by saying, "I know who I am."

We have to learn to forgive ourselves for thinking those thoughts that would separate us from this God expression. Thank God for the power of forgiving, for knowing we can forgive, and come back to that inner self, that inner Spirit of Truth. When we come back to that inner self, we realize, like the man who lay by the pool, we too can pick up our bed and walk; we too can pick up our minds and be renewed and step out again in faith and belief.

Take the Time . . .

When you get up each morning, take a few moments to be still. Take a few moments to be thankful. Take a few moments to be integrated with the entire universe. Some of us never see flowers. Some of us never hear birds sing. Some of us never see rabbits. We never see animal life. We never see anything but what we are putting on and where we are going. But, oh, if you would just take a few moments and be integrated with the wholeness of the universe, you would find out that you are one with everything. There is nothing beautiful in this world of which you are not a part.

Take some time each day to read something inspirational, to lift your consciousness so that when you go out, you go out knowing that it is a great day. Know that when you step out into the world, you step out as one not only filled with love and joy but as one who can bring that love and joy alive in someone else's life. When you go out into the world, you can reach out and touch someone, no matter what color, what ethnic background, what religion. You can reach out and realize that you are one with everything and everybody.

Of course we have a right to our differences of opinion. But over and beyond any differences, there is still a Oneness, an inclusive Presence that exists and helps us to realize that *healing takes place whenever any of us chooses to be his or her own ticket.* That's what it's all about, for there comes a time when the teachers, the preachers, the practitioners, the friends are not there. Then what do you do? Who do you lean on? Where do you go for help?

All the people you might choose to follow are there for a given time for a given purpose. Their most important function is to help you know that you have been given the power to touch yourself, to bless yourself, to heal yourself. You've been given the power to know that no matter what the appearance, no matter what the situation may be—whether it's the healing of your body, the search for a job, the strengthening of a relationship, or just getting to know yourself—no matter what, *you have the power to heal and bless yourself.*

This ticket, the ticket to your health, is one ticket you don't have to buy. It's one ticket you don't have to pay for. It is yours by divine right, because you are the very essence of your own wholeness.

AFFIRMATIONS

1. *I praise the life of God flowing freely through my entire body.*

2. *I forgive myself for all the mistakes I have made. I uproot every unloving thought in my mind.*

3. *As my thoughts are harmonious, my life is harmonious.*

4. *My heart is not troubled or afraid.*

5. *My heart is filled with love, with gratitude.*

6. *My soul is at peace.*

7. *I surrender my fears.*

8. *I close my mind to things in the external and focus on the mighty healing power of God, healing every cell and organ to its perfect image.*

9. *I praise God for restoring, renewing, revitalizing, and healing my body.*

10. *Love is in charge of my life and I am made whole.*

11. *The life of God flows freely through my entire being, cleansing, healing, and restoring me.*

12. *I have faith in God as the one Presence at work in my body making me whole.*

13. *I look past appearances and symptoms and I am alive and alight with the glory of God.*

CHAPTER TWELVE

✳

Addictions

I'm excited about this chapter because I can share with you, my reader, another exciting experience I've had.

I spoke at a conference where I talked about my relationship to a family member. Lillian Desjardins, codirector of Le Pavilion, was the second speaker. After hearing me she invited me to be the guest of her and her husband, Gilles (Executive director), at their center in Montreal, Canada. The center offers psychotherapy service that includes group and individual therapy. I smiled, thanked her, and went on my "merry way." I should indicate here that her topic was about "co-dependency," which I heard but "tuned out"—certainly it did not apply to me.

During the year, I met many ministers who had gone to the center. The reports were always positive. A year later, I reached a point of no return with my family member, my church work, and with me. It was as if I couldn't satisfy myself or anyone else. My tolerance level was extremely low. I am the founder of a wonderful ministry that has grown in membership for twenty-three years beyond my wildest dreams. Demands are made on me as a minister twenty-four hours a day. Sometimes, more often I forget to take care of my personal needs. Even when I chose to accept an engagement to speak outside our church, I found myself dealing with guilt. Sometimes I wanted to just take one Sunday off for a weekend holiday, but I just believed I couldn't and shouldn't. Having just completed the construction of a new 1,200-seat, twelve-classroom, three-million-dollar facility, I deserved a rest. I was stressed out, burnt out, and just plain tired. Finally, I reached out to the Le Pavilion center and the invitation was still open.

I had forgotten that the material I received earlier clearly stated it was a recovery center. Well, at least I could recover from stress. I left home going to rest, relax, sleep late, eat well, etc. Can you imagine my surprise when I arrived at the center and discovered some of the above was true and that I was in a structured program of classes with thirty other strangers who had a variety of addictions. At my first class meeting, as introductions were being given, I heard:

"I'm a sex addict."

"My problem is food."

"I've been on drugs."

"I am an alcoholic."

"Co-dependence has affected every part of my life."

"My family had a conference and decided I should be here."

"Gambling is my game."

"I'm a workaholic."

"I'm out of control in my relationships."

Well, when they got to me I emphatically said, "My name is Barbara King and I don't know *why* I am here! Addictions? Not me!"

Well, that was the beginning of a new journey for me. After speaking with Lillian, I found out that I was co-dependent not only with my family member but also with my church members.

I proceeded to discover that my co-dependency was manifesting with my family member in addictive behaviors such as compulsive caretaking and my inability to say no. I discovered that I was a control addict who could not let go. A lot of enabling brings a lot of pain, and I was addicted to suffering and pain. All of this was making me feel lonely, guilty and over-responsible.

Furthermore, to my total surprise, I discovered that I was caretaking my congregation way over the call of my vocation. In my church I was a workaholic and perfectionist and I am now in recovery. As the program was unfolding I remembered reading somewhere that we are an "addictive society." I started having a deep understanding of this statement.

The environment in which I was discovering the layers of my pain and dysfunction was safe, loving, and compassionate. Please understand here that for me, the minister, the caregiver, to allow myself to be so vulnerable with people I did not know, was the key. My openness to their needs and theirs to mine were simply the healing I needed. My surrender was allowing others to take care of me.

What I did not know is how our egos are structured. A part of me is my human self, my personality, my exterior values, and the other part of me is my identity, my higher self and my inner values.

At the Pavilion I discovered what went wrong with my ego and how it became diseased. All human beings are driven by some basic needs:

1. Physical needs: food, shelter, etc.
2. Need to belong, i.e., need to love and be loved
3. Need for power and manageability
4. Need for freedom
5. Need for fun

When these basic needs are not adequately met, especially in our formative years, there is disorder, and sickness follows in the form of a diseased ego. The main characteristics of the diseased ego are an exaggerated importance of self and an unrealistic notion of self. Both of these will trigger an unrealistic notion of control . . . and denial is born. That in turn produces negative emotions such as fear, anger, insecurity, guilt, grief, futility, shame and solitude (in the sense of loneliness and isolation). I certainly could identify with this.

If in addition our original imprint comes from a dysfunctional family background (such as mine), the basic needs as well as feelings will be denied and suppressed. That causes the ego's negative emotions to turn into character defects.

Therefore, anger produces resentments, demands, intolerance, blame, vengeance and manipulation.

Fear produces rejection of self and others, envy, jealousy, impatience, inadequacy and false pride—all of this resulting in very low self-esteem.

Just to name a few.

I started having an awakening.

Yes, many times I said to my congregation to repeat: "I am a spiritual being having a human experience." Now I know how true this statement is, but more than that I truly understand my human experience—my diseased ego leading into addictions.

Through the introspective work at the Pavilion I identified the emotional pressure my ego was causing, and I understood that co-dependency was the inevitable path. I saw how I had to medicate my feelings compulsively with food, work, people, etc. I had to alter my mood.

I discovered that substance abuse, food and sex addictions, gambling and compulsive spending, work, etc., are but fifteen percent of the problem. They are the outer manifestation of the inner turmoil. Fifty-five percent of the problem is our diseased ego, our co-dependence and our dysfunctional imprint. Three core addictions define the diseased ego the best:

Power/control addiction
Security addiction = the not-enough syndrome
Sensation addiction = let's kill the pain now!

I began to identify with much of the above, as you the reader probably have. The question was, What is the bottom line in this addiction stuff? Why didn't we each go to a separate program to heal our needs—sex addiction, food addiction, co-dependency, etc.?

All of our addictions were coming from the same source—our diseased ego, which we could take the steps to heal through our spiritual identity and be made whole.

We inventoried our life experiences and the word *dysfunction* took on a deeper meaning. For all of us our families and environments affected us in such a way that we only repeated the behavior patterns they gave to us. Out of anger for what they did came the need for forgiveness of family members, as well as of self. With compassion I understood that everyone in my past has done the best they knew how under the circumstances, and so did I.

It was exciting to see the healing process as we worked through the shadow and into the light. I was offered a system and steps to process the dysfunction, to monitor my behavior and to empower my spiritual identity in all its beauty, wisdom and love.

This was a true homecoming. Yes, coming home to the precious in me that was created in the image and likeness of God. I felt awakened and alive.

What impressed me most was that first of all I shared daily

with people who were representative of all of the above. They are really just "ordinary people" caught up in the past history of their dysfunctional families, usually characterized by:

1. death of a parent or family member
2. chronic illnesses
3. divorce
4. alcoholism or drug abuse
5. parents or children of alcoholics
6. food or sex addict
7. abuse: physical, sexual, emotional, intellectual, spiritual, violent
8. emotionally absent or emotionally overbearing parent
9. parents who were workaholics filled with security, power, control, and sensation addictions.

With all of the above and so much more, the bottom line is surrender—surrender to your spiritual nature, your God-self, your higher power. Realize you can't do it alone. Somehow we have to come to the realization that in our world today, we are so out of balance. We cannot survive without physical, mental, emotional, and spiritual unity. We must understand that our emotions affect our minds and bodies. We need to see our spiritual nature as the healing balance and begin to use it through prayer, meditation, affirmation, and participation in support groups, whether it be the church or self-help organizations. I saw lives transformed at the center once the inner connection was made to God within. As one member of our group said very boldly, "I'm so glad to know God is within me as well as omnipresent, omniscient, and omnipotent." "What the world needs now is love (God) sweet love (God)." Our spiritual growth is contingent upon our practicing the twelve steps to recovery. They are:

12 STEPS

1.) We admitted we were powerless over our diseased ego— that our lives had become unmanageable.

2.) We came to believe that a power greater than ourselves could restore us to sanity.

3.) We made a decision to turn our will and our lives over to the care of God as we understood Him (Her).

4.) We made a searching and fearless moral inventory of ourselves.

5.) We admitted to God, to ourselves, and to another human being the exact nature of our wrongs.

6.) We were entirely ready to have God remove all these defects of character.

7.) We humbly asked Him to remove our shortcomings.

8.) We made a list of all persons we had harmed, and became willing to make amends to them all.

9.) We made direct amends to such people wherever possible, except when to do so would injure them or others.

10.) We continued to take personal inventory and when we were wrong, promptly admitted it.

11.) We sought through prayer and meditation to improve our conscious contact with God as we understood Him, praying only for knowledge of His will for us and the power to carry that out.

12.) Having had a spiritual awakening as the result of these steps, we tried to carry this message to others, and to practice these principles in all our affairs.

Not only did I work on my own addictions, but I learned so much that will help me in my pastoring. I am more sensitive to the needs of my members and friends who come for counseling and to our worship services, classes, and workshops.

I am in recovery and so is my church, with whom I shared the good news about my twenty-eight-day journey. After all, they are my family. I recently read an article explaining that recovery is a never-ending process of becoming and being. The article is entitled "Recovery Is Letting Go":

To "let go" does not mean to stop caring, it means I can't do it for someone else.

To "let go" is not to cut myself off, it's the realization I can't control another.

To "let go" is not to enable, but to allow learning from natural consequences.

To "let go" is to admit powerlessness, which means the outcome is not in my hands.

To "let go" is not to try to change or blame another, it's to make the most of myself.

To "let go" is not to care for, but to care about.

To "let go" is not to fix, but to be supportive.

To "let go" is not to judge, but to allow another to be a human being.

To "let go" is not to be in the middle arranging all the outcomes, but to allow others to affect their own destinies.

To "let go" is not to deny, but to accept.

To "let go" is not to nag, scold, or argue, but instead to search out my own shortcomings and correct them.

To "let go" is not to adjust everything to my desires, but to take each day as it comes, and cherish myself in it.

To "let go" is not to regret the past, but to grow and live for the future.

To "let go" is to fear less and love more.

(Anonymous)

I am still in the process of becoming. Thank God I'm not where I used to be. Accept this chapter as my testimony—"God is Good all the time." Le Pavilion will be relocating to the U.S. from Montreal, Canada, in 1995. I look forward to their seminars and workshops for my continued growth.

AFFIRMATIONS

1. *God within me now sets me free from my compulsive craving and need to continue this addiction.*
2. *I do not have to look to anything outside myself for pleasure and satisfaction.*
3. *I refuse to allow my peers to influence me in doing anything that is not right for me.*
4. *I do not have to agree with or patronize others to gain popularity.*
5. *Within me there is no sense of insecurity, inferiority or depression.*
6. *I do not have to prove anything to anyone.*
7. *The joy of the Lord is my strength.*
8. *I now place my attention on Spirit within me to satisfy my every need and desire.*
9. *My body is the temple of the living God and God is in control.*
10. *I have faith in God in me to set me free from my addiction.*
11. *Within me is all the strength, the courage, the love, the wisdom I need to overcome my co-dependency.*
12. *I now make a conscious decision to release the desire and compulsive obsession of using drugs, in the name and through the mighty power of Jesus Christ.*
13. *Almighty Father with whom nothing is impossible, I surrender (name) and this thing called (name of addiction) over to you; I of myself can do nothing.*
14. *Today I make a conscious decision to lay my burden down.*

CHAPTER THIRTEEN

*

Transitions (Death) and Beyond

I don't often go back and look at notes of past sermons, but I did go through my files one day and discovered that it had been many years since I had spoken from the pulpit on the subject of death. It was during a time when some heavy emotions were being felt in the city of Atlanta. This sadness, this grief, this mourning was caused by a series of brutal, puzzling murders of children. Death is difficult enough for most people to accept under any circumstances; murder makes it all the harder.

Yet it is our basic, underlying attitude toward death that causes the greatest difficulty. That attitude must be changed if we are to accept death for what it is, for as Jesus said, "Neither is new wine put into old wineskins; if it is, the skins burst, and the wine is spilled, and the skins are destroyed; but new wine is put into fresh wineskins, and so both are preserved" (Matthew 9:17). These words suggest that one reason we don't progress spiritually is that we're still holding on to old conflicts and old beliefs that bind and place limitations on us and keep us from enjoying the fullness of life that God is, that God has promised. This fullness of life is what Paul referred to when he said, "For in Him we live, and move, and have our being" (Acts 17: 28).

But when you listen and begin to believe in God's truth, then the old beliefs have to go. Two ideas cannot occupy the mind at the same time. So a new understanding of death will cause the old fear of death to move out of your consciousness. *This concept of death being something we have to fear is a human thought.* It is not God's plan, for life is eternal. Jesus made this very plain when he said, "I am come that they might have life, and that they might have it more abundantly" (John 10:10). He didn't say, "that they might have a little piece of life." He said *abundantly*. If you and I are not having life abundantly, it is because we are not living by the spiritual Law.

For example, as children many of us ended our day by praying, "Now I lay me down to sleep; I pray the Lord my soul to keep. If I should die before I wake, I pray the Lord my soul to take." And we believed in that prayer and went on to sleep. We didn't worry about waking up, because we knew that we were going to get up and go back to our toys, our games, our friends, and our familiar surroundings.

Think about that. As children, we believed in abundant life. This is what Jesus meant when he said we have to become as little children. The mind of a child is so much more teachable than that of an adult. As children, we prayed that nightly prayer with power. So why, as adults, do we fear death?

Some of us don't even say the word. Say it: *death*. Say it aloud: *death*. There are so many folks walking around worrying about dying that they're not living. Most of us are dead on our feet because we don't realize that life is consciousness. Such people are living only in the physical. But *there is that divineness in each of us, there is that Spirit which cannot die.* Since that's the case, what's so wrong with shedding the physical body when we know we're going on to something greater? New wine is put into *fresh* wineskins!

Life, the Center of Our Being

Let's turn to the intellect for a moment, for that too is part of our God-given self. From an intellectual perspective, death can be viewed metaphysically. Metaphysics is simply a systematic study of the science of Being—that which transcends or goes beyond the physical. Now, one who practices metaphysics, one skilled in the science of Being, is a metaphysician, a student and teacher of the laws of Spirit. In the New Thought movement, we're all metaphysicians, because we go beyond the physical to enable us to get away from the human limitations and embrace our spiritual selves. By working at the spiritual level, we behold the Spirit of God in us, God incarnate in us as life, as love, as wisdom, as truth, as abundance, as prosperity—all the attributes of God flowing through our spiritual selves.

To illustrate this, suppose we draw a circle to represent the spiritual self. Then, around that circle, let's draw another circle, so that our illustration looks like this:

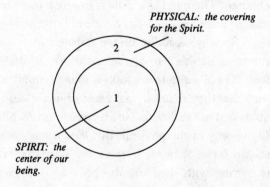

PHYSICAL: *the covering for the Spirit.*

SPIRIT: *the center of our being.*

The inner circle, numbered 1, is that part of us which is like our Creator, for, as we know, we are made in the image and likeness of God; and that image is a spiritual image. Circle number 2, the outer circle, is the environment in which we exist. This environment is made up of many things, including where we live, how we live, what influences us, and so forth. This outer circle, in fact, is what we usually refer to when we say "life," for this is our conscious experience. So there is an inner self of us and an outer self. Recognizing this is the key to everything we do, the key to life and death. That inner self, to use Paul's words again, is where we live, move, and have our being. But that outer circle surrounds the inner and acts as an inhibitor that keeps us from letting God work through us. Here in this outer circle are our hang-ups, our mistakes, our false beliefs, our friends, and all things physical and material. Many of us spend all our conscious time and energy in that outer circle. Even in the face of death we are in that outer circle, worrying about who's going to get the car, who's going to be wearing my clothes, how will the folks survive without me, will my wife/husband remarry?

But I want to tell you that *living constantly in the outer circle creates a fear of death.* How? Because we spend so much time worrying about the outer, about our material possessions, about our human relationships, that we can't enjoy them, because we know that sooner or later death will take us away from them. Fortunately, most of us eventually reach a point in life where we begin to place less emphasis on the outer and more on the inner. At that point, we begin to seek answers to many concerns, including our fear of death.

What we find, though, is that we can't explain everything. Even God is incomprehensible to us. We really don't fully understand God; we're just picking at what we think we know to be true. No one can really explain it all. But one thing we *do* come to understand as we begin to seek God's Truth is that immortality is a characteristic of God. And since we all have within us that inner circle, that spiritual image of God, then it follows that immortality must also be a characteristic of each of us. With this understanding comes yet another understanding: *when the soul goes through the transition we call death, it is not dying but simply giving up a physical expression to move on to an even greater, more glorious expression.*

Dealing with a Loved One's Transition

I believe that our loved ones who have passed on are as close to us as we think them to be, for again, life is consciousness. If a loved one has gone out of the physical body, you will find that when you draw into your consciousness thoughts about that loved one, then nothing is between the two of you except a sort of transparent barrier that can be overcome by thought. There are numerous instances of research by doctors and scientists on life after death. People have told of "dying" on the operating table, for instance, and journeying through what they describe as dark tunnels to light. One lady said, "I didn't see a figure of God. What I saw and felt was so much love that I had to make up in my mind that I wanted to come back and be with my children. And I got myself together and came on back."

Elisabeth Kübler-Ross, one of the foremost authorities on the question of life after death, has worked with a number of cancer patients and, through her research, has helped millions make the transition into their next cycle. She says that death is simply the shedding of the physical body, like a butterfly coming out of a cocoon. It is a transition into a higher state of consciousness, in which you continue to perceive and to understand and to be able to grow. The only thing you lose is something you don't need anymore, your physical body. It's like putting away your winter coat when spring comes.

So there is no separation except in your human thought. And many times when someone leaves a physical body, we go through the sadness and the mourning because we don't want to release the person. Our human feelings take over. But in our spiritual mind, we know that the life of that person is still expressing with the Father in its own way. Once we become aware of this truth, the grief, the mourning, and the daily sense of loss will move away from us.

Another thing we have to realize is that sometimes our loved ones want to release the physical body. Perhaps they are only continuing in this existence because they know that we are not ready for them to go, and so they hang on in order to give us time to make the adjustment. But such a person will find a way to release the body, whether through illness, accident, or by act of his own hand. That's another reason that it does us little good to indulge in excessive grief—we don't know what's on our loved ones' consciousness before they leave here.

So many times when I deliver a eulogy—I call them "words of life"—I say to families, "That is not your loved one in that casket. That's just a body. Your loved one has released the physical, but at a spiritual level, he still exists." What I'm saying is that God receives His own back to Him. Life doesn't end; it continues. Life goes back to life. There's no breaking the cycle of life. **What we have to break is our old habit of thinking about death as something dreadful.**

And when a loved one moves into another cycle of life, more than ever do we need to remember that our Father, a God of love, so takes care of His creation that as we move to the next experience, that same God of love is right there. What the survivors have to do is to hold fast to the truth of Jesus' teachings about resurrection, about life being eternal, about life being abundant. And the survivors owe it to themselves to continue to take every day as a day of joy and to turn their thoughts to living, as God intended them to do.

What's It Like on the "Other Side"?

Now, I'm not going to argue with anybody about the streets of gold. If that's your belief about what you'll encounter on the "other side," that's all right. We're all at different levels of consciousness. Didn't Jesus say, "In my Father's house are many mansions" (John 14:2)? I only know that in this physical body there's that which takes place in me which is so wonderful and so peaceful and just downright exciting that I *know* I have nothing to fear when I move on to my next experience.

A lady sitting next to me on an airplane said to me, after we'd been talking for a while, "Boy, I wonder what *you're* going to be a little later on." I said, "Honey, I don't know; but whatever it is, it's bound to be good!" You see, I *feel* good about myself. I'm so excited about using the Truths of God and seeing the results that I just keep saying, "Well, Father, what's next?" Whether it's here or there, it doesn't matter. Just the idea of expression, of living and enjoying life is enough. Feeling this kind of joy on this conscious, physical level, I begin to comprehend what the apostle meant when he said, "It doth not yet appear what we shall be: but we know that, when He shall appear, we shall be like Him; for we shall see Him as He is" (1 John 3:2).

So what we need to realize is that *all* experience, including that we call death, is part of eternity. And eternity is right now. You've got all the eternity that you're ever going to have, right here, right now. The past and the future come together in the now. And death is no more than a graduation from one level of experience to another.

Work with yourself to know this truth, and fear of death cannot stay in your mind. It's your attitude about it that makes it fearful, because death itself is just a transition. Spirit *cannot die.* Yes, eventually we all face the experience of physical death. But even then, God gives us the strength to grow, to look beyond the moment and know that there is something more—abundantly more—for us to experience.

With spiritual maturity, our prayer can progress from the "Now I lay me down to sleep" of childhood to a twenty-four-hour-a-day awareness that God is always the keeper of our soul. As James Dillet Freeman so beautifully expresses it in his "Prayer for Protection":

> The light of God surrounds me;
> The love of God enfolds me;
> The power of God protects me;
> The presence of God watches over me;
> Wherever I am, God is.

I'm also including in this chapter a second poem by Mr. Freeman, "I Am There." I have used it often at memorial services and the words are comforting to those who hear it.

I Am There

> Do you need Me?
> I am there.
> You cannot see Me, yet I am the light you see by.
> You cannot hear Me, yet I speak through your
> voice.

You cannot feel Me, yet I am the power at work in
  your hands.

I am at work, though you do not understand My ways.

I am at work, though you do not recognize My
  works.

I am not strange visions. I am not mysteries.

Only in absolute stillness, beyond self, can you
  know Me as I am, and then but as a feeling and
  a faith.

Yet I am there. Yet I hear. Yet I answer.

When you need Me, I am there.

Even if you deny Me, I am there.

Even when you feel most alone, I am there.

Even in your fears, I am there.

Even in your pain, I am there.

I am there when you pray and when you do not
  pray.

I am in you, and you are in Me.

Only in your mind can you feel separate from Me,
  for only in your mind are the mists of "yours"
  and "mine."

Yet only with your mind can you know Me and
  experience Me.

Empty your heart of empty fears.

When you get yourself out of the way, I am there.

You can of yourself do nothing, but I can do all.

And I am in all.

Though you may not see the good, good is there,
  for I am there.

I am there because I have to be, because I am.

Only in Me does the world have meaning; only out
  of Me does the world take form; only because
  of Me does the world go forward.

I am the law on which the movement of the stars
and the growth of living cells are founded.

I am the love that is the law's fulfilling. I am
assurance. I am peace. I am oneness. I am the
law that you can live by. I am the love that you
can cling to. I am your assurance. I am your
peace. I am one with you. I am.

Though you fail to find Me, I do not fail you.

Though your faith in Me is unsure, My faith in you
never wavers, because I know you, because I
love you.

Beloved, I am there.

AFFIRMATION
The 23rd Psalm

The Lord is my shepherd;
I shall not want.
He maketh me to lie down in green pastures:
He leadeth me beside the still waters.
He restoreth my soul: He leadeth me in the
paths of righteousness for His name's sake.
Yea, though I walk through the valley of the shadow
of death, I will fear no evil:
for Thou art with me; Thy rod and Thy staff
they comfort me.
Thou preparest a table before me in the presence of
mine enemies: Thou anointest my head with oil;
my cup runneth over.
Surely goodness and mercy shall follow me all the days of
my life: and I will dwell in the house of the Lord forever.

CHAPTER FOURTEEN

When You've Done All That You Can

Let go and let God. This affirmation means that there comes a time when human effort must give over to God effort. It is also directly related to the commandment to remember the Sabbath and keep it holy. When we think of the word *Sabbath,* we know that it means to rest, to withdraw from all activity. For the Hebrews the number seven was considered a time to rest and to move away from six days of work or continuous activity. Many Christians, however, tend to feel that the word *Sabbath* applies only to Sunday. But if we look at the word's true meaning, then we see that whenever we cease our outer activity and choose instead to rest and to reflect on Spirit or things that are like God, then we are observing a Sabbath.

This is so true for working people! How many people, for instance, work on the day we call Sunday? If they are religious people and take *Sabbath* to mean Sunday, then they might feel that they are sinning because they are at work and not at church. But when the church as an institution has weekday services and weekday activities, then whatever day those who work on Sunday have free—Monday, Tuesday, whatever—they should be able to go to their places of worship and still share in a service activity if they want to observe the Sabbath in that sense. So what we're really talking about when we refer to "the Sabbath" is the stopping of all the pressures that we're under and the recognition that it's time to really go to the Father.

Another Kind of Sabbath

Now this concept of observing the Sabbath doesn't apply just to the work you get paid for or to the physical labor or other work you do with your hands. It also applies to the mental work you do in your attempt to solve problems or overcome challenges. These efforts can be every bit as tiring as physical labor, and they too deserve a Sabbath.

For instance, suppose you've been working with a problem for some time, or suppose it's a problem that you're facing for the first time. Either way, your first step is to recognize the problem for what it is—a temporary condition that you have the power to control and therefore need not be frightened by.

In the Scriptures, for example, we find the story of Jesus crossing a lake with the disciples after a long day of healing and teaching and working continuously. While they were crossing, a great storm arose, and the disciples became very fearful and woke Jesus up. "Are you just going to let us drown?" they asked him. Well, the first thing Jesus did was to rebuke the waves and tell them to be still, which they did. Then he said to the disciples, "Why are ye so fearful? How is it that ye have no faith?" (Mark 4:40).

What does this say to *us*? Many of you right now are going through experiences—you're worrying; some of you have walked the floor all night long. All the walking the floor, all the worrying still has not solved the problem. That worry, that problem, is just like the wind and the waves that frightened the disciples. They put their faith in the winds and the waves and the rolling and the movement. Jesus told them, *Put your faith in a living presence. I'm here. I'm in the boat; and I'm symbolizing the sonship of the One Presence, the One Power, God.*

If you place your faith in that Presence or in Jesus as the representative of It, then you will not be disturbed by the wind and the waves—mental storms, in other words. When unfavorable things are happening to you, the first thing you need to do is recognize that God is all-powerful—the only power in the universe. That's the first thought you have to grasp when in need.

The Still, Small Voice

So now you've confronted the problem with a calm mind and you've recognized that God in you gives you the overcoming power. Perhaps you will immediately know of some steps you can take toward working out the problem. Your life experiences and what we call "mother wit" should suggest to you some obvious things that you can do. If you find that you're going to be late with your house payment, for instance, you will of course want to contact your mortgage holder.

But what about this "mother wit" that I speak of? What is that? In Proverbs, the second chapter, sixth verse, we find these words: "For the Lord giveth wisdom: out of His mouth cometh knowledge and understanding." This wisdom is the God-given faculty of intuition; it's what is meant by "the still, small voice of God," which moves through us consciously. When we open ourselves up to listen, to receive, to dwell on the Truths of God, then we get within us a flow of thought that is beyond intellect.

Intellect is acquired knowledge, knowledge that is learned from teachers, books, newspapers, or any other outside source.

But mother wit, as I say, is the wisdom of God; it's what you feel when you have a "hunch" about something. **So if you're still faced with the problem after doing everything you consciously can to solve it, then take a Sabbath by getting still in mind and body.** No matter how many factors are involved, you'll find that in the stillness, the quietness, a flow of thought will come through your mind. When that flow begins, capture it, hold on to it, and see it as the wisdom of God.

Remember that there is another dimension to you that's greater than your humanness: there's that Spirit of the living God which speaks to your soul, speaks to your heart all the time, giving you guidance and direction. It is left up to you whether you will use it. Get still and listen for the answer. It may not come immediately, but that's why you are taking a Sabbath from the problem. While you are waiting, all the details are being ironed out; whoever you have to make contact with is being made ready to see you; whatever resources you may need are being made available to you. Thus, you see, the wisdom of God is constantly working through you so that when the time comes to act, you'll know *what* to do, *when* to do it, and *how* to do it.

One reason we often can't express the wisdom of God is that we're very fearful. We might think that others know what's right but that we don't. Many people, before they decide anything, go and get everybody's opinion. It's all right to go to people for advice. But before you do, get still, go to God, and then to the person that you are directed to go to. Sometimes off the top of the head, as we say, you can't think of the right person. But if you take a Sabbath at that point—get still, forget about it, go to lunch, whatever—a name will just flow through your consciousness when you least expect it. And you'll know immediately that that's the person for you to seek out. I have found that when such a name comes through or an idea is revealed to me, *it is* the perfect answer.

Never try to force a solution to a problem, in other words. Every time you get fearful and anxious about what you ought to do, take a Sabbath. Get still and talk to God. Talk to that Presence, that Power, that Spirit within, which is your teacher. Hold a conversation just as though you were talking with someone face-to-face. Some people might say you're crazy if you talk to yourself, but don't you believe it! It's good to talk to yourself, to just kind of feel yourself out and get out all the doubt and fear. Don't depend on someone else to decide what is right for you. Accept the recommendations, accept the comments. Then get busy and make a decision based on *your* judgment, and stand by that decision.

One Day at a Time

Know that your wisdom faculty operates discriminatingly and with good judgment. You can look at things and know whether or not they're good for you; you can make decisions with God's guidance and know that they're the right decisions. Some of us get into trouble financially, emotionally, in our relationships—in so many aspects of our lives—because we try to force solutions, when all we need do is let go and let God. We get in such a hurry! Everything must be done right now, every problem must be solved instantly! But if we would just slow down, take Sabbaths when we need them, and recognize that we have a lifetime to do all the things we want to do—then we'd be happy to take life just one day at a time and to take as many Sabbaths as we need.

Someone wrote a song called "One Day at a Time, Sweet Jesus," and oh, how true that is! If you'll just take one day, one challenge, and look at it and work with it a little piece at a time, you'll find that wisdom will teach you that when one door closes, another is always ready to open. Instead of being disheartened by closing doors, you'll realize, *this upset has been for my highest good.* When you begin to live in that consciousness, you will be able to look beyond appearances and to avoid panic and unwise decisions. God has built this capacity into you by giving you access to His wisdom and has provided you with a way to reach that wisdom—the Sabbath.

Jesus is the perfect example. After so many days of labor, as described at the beginning of this chapter, He did not hesitate to take that period of rest—that's why He and the disciples were crossing the lake: to reach a place where they could rest. He would stop His labor to reenergize, to get back in touch with that living presence called God.

The farmer is another example. He collects the seed, he plants it, he waters it. But the real working of the seed is God. It's God who makes the seed what it was intended to be in the beginning. The sprout, the stem, the leaves—everything that grows does so through the power of Spirit. And this is how it is with our ideas and the solutions to our problems. Whenever you are told to let go and let God, the idea is not that you should just give up, but that you pray about it and let God direct and guide you to right action. Any time you get to a point where you don't know what to do, stop and take a period of rest.

Making a Sabbath Work for you

Here are some steps for taking an effective Sabbath and developing your wisdom faculty:

1. Have periods of meditation and prayer. Begin your day by taking at least fifteen minutes to listen, to just get still. If you have to start with five minutes and work your way up to fifteen, it's okay. Find a technique to help you attain this stillness. It may be beautiful music or may be poetry; it may be the Scriptures. Whatever it is, take time to meditate on something that is beautiful and that will lift your consciousness above what you know you'll be facing during the day. While you're in this meditative state, speak the Truth. Say, *God, you are in control of my day. I give it over to You so that Your wisdom will come through me in everything I do.* Then repeat this period of meditation at midday and at night.

2. Listen for inspiration from Spirit. The Scriptures say, *"Be still and know that I am God."* I just went on a trip, for instance, and so many ideas came flowing through my mind because I took time to listen for them.

3. Let your mind dwell on the qualities of God. What are those qualities? Love, sharing, giving, understanding, patience, tolerance—all the qualities that we love when we see them in other people.

As the apostle Paul said, "Whatsoever things are true, whatsoever things are honest, whatsoever things are just, whatsoever things are pure, whatsoever things are lovely, whatsoever things are of good report . . . think on these things" (Philippians 4:8). Those are the qualities of God.

4. Act on the inspiration received. When you receive the inspiration, don't just hold it and not use it. Maybe you and your coworkers have been wrestling with something technical and suddenly you get a flow of thought. Act on it, because it comes straight from the one Source: God the Good omnipotent.

Whatever problem you're facing, do the best that you can

do toward solving it. Then don't be afraid to take a Sabbath—
let go and let God. Somewhere along the line, the consciousness
of opposition—whether within you or without—will give way
in your favor.

CHAPTER FIFTEEN

*

Where Do I Go From Here?

$\mathcal{A}$ few months ago, I went to speak at a prestigious church in a major city. The minister took me out to dinner the evening before and impressed upon me that I was speaking to a very important congregation, that his people were very wealthy and highly intellectual. He wanted me to know what I would be facing the next morning when I stood in his pulpit. You see, at this particular church, no person of color had ever stood in the pulpit. In fact, there were no persons of color in this particular congregation. And there I was, a person of color, and what's more, a woman minister!

Well, I looked at him, I listened to him. He asked me if I had any comments. I said, "No, I have no comment to make because I know that the Spirit of the Lord will give me a message." He said that the church bulletin was being run off that night and that he would like to know the title of my message so that he could include it. I said, "I can't tell you, because nothing is coming through to me at this time. So will you permit me to just be myself and just let Spirit work through me when

I come in the morning?" He agreed to this.

When I arrived the next morning and took my seat by the pulpit, I looked out at the congregation. Sure enough, everybody was looking directly at me, and my first thought was "Wow! Father, are You sure I'm in the right place? Maybe I don't measure up after all." And then the second thought came: *Be still and know that I am God.*

When the time came for me to speak, I stood silently for a moment. Then I said, "You know, there are so many of us who have reached what we call the pinnacle of success. We're in the right church; we're sitting in the right pew; we have the right friends; we've earned our degrees; we have the right job, the right salary; we're generally in the right position in life."

Then I said, "But do you know what I'm finding out in my travels and in my work? That for many of us who have reached the so-called pinnacle of success, there still appears to be something missing from our lives."

This brings me to the question I want to raise in this concluding chapter. Once you have it all, where do you go from there? In Mark, the tenth chapter, verses seventeen to twenty-five, there is an incident between Jesus and a rich young ruler that illustrates what I'm saying.

> And when he was gone forth into the way, there came one running, and kneeled to him, and asked him, "Good Master, what shall I do that I may inherit eternal life?"
>
> And Jesus said unto him, "Why callest thou me good? There is none good but one, that is, God.
>
> "Thou knowest the commandments, Do not commit adultery, Do not kill, Do not steal, Do not bear false witness, Defraud not, Honor thy father and mother."

And he answered and said unto him, "Master, all these have I observed from my youth."

Then Jesus beholding him loved him, and said unto him, "One thing thou lackest: go thy way, sell whatsoever thou hast, and give to the poor, and thou shalt have treasure in heaven: and come, take up the cross, and follow me."

And he was sad at that saying, and went away grieved: for he had great possessions.

And Jesus looked round about, and saith unto His disciples, "How hardly shall they that have riches enter into the kingdom of God!"

And the disciples were astonished at His words. But Jesus answereth again, and saith unto them, "Children, how hard is it for them that trust in riches to enter into the kingdom of God!

"It is easier for a camel to go through the eye of a needle, than for a rich man to enter into the kingdom of God."

Where Is Your Trust?

Now, we don't see in this conversation where Jesus made any statement that it's a sin to be rich. That's not the essence of the conversation. Our Father is rich, and we are the heirs of a rich universe. Furthermore, God is no respecter of person, by which I mean that it doesn't matter *who* we are or what we have—we are all equal in His sight. So all of us have the opportunity to draw upon the abundance of God, which is everywhere equally present.

But in talking about the young man, Jesus used a key word: *trust*—specifically, in this case, trust in riches, in the material. There are so many of us who are pushing, who are moving, who are striving totally to satisfy our needs through material possessions. What's happening in many such cases is that the inner self, the spiritual part of us, is not at peace. That is the implication of this message. Jesus said to the young man, all right, you've kept the commandments, you have everything that anybody could desire; but there's something else beyond keeping the commandments. And that is knowing within yourself that if the material is lost to you, you still have the Spirit of the living God.

Whatever moves away from you or out of your life, as Jesus explained to His disciples, can be multiplied a hundredfold by the Lord, because God works through each of us. And if we are willing to put God first in all our material quests, then we don't have anything to worry about. The young man just couldn't see that. He really wanted to experience God, he really wanted to know what it was to have that full salvation. But he could not give up the material.

Strive for Balance

Psychologists and scientists have long spoken of left-brained and right-brained people. Those who are dominated by the left side of their brains are the intellectuals; they are the ones who are very much concerned about analysis, about criticism, about looking at things thoroughly, seeing to the very point of a thing's inception. Then there are the predominantly right-brained individuals who are more into the intuitive, who are aesthetes, who are the artists, and who look for beauty.

There is nothing wrong with being either left-brained or right-brained; but we need to strive for a balance between the two, a good combination of both. Clearly, the young man in the parable was caught up with his left brain. His position in life spoke of the intellect, of thinking, of planning, of knowing how to manage his resources to achieve great wealth. But his right brain, his intuitiveness, his desire for the Spirit was also coming up, and he didn't know how to balance the two. So rather than make that step to balance himself, he chose to leave Jesus and say, "I don't think I can accept what you're telling me."

How many of us have reached that point? In so many ways we might feel that we have it all, that we don't need anything or anybody, that we "have arrived." And yet, deep within, most of us who are making those kinds of assertions are also hurting; we're in pain, confused, anxious, worried. Why? Because we will not allow the intuitiveness, the God-self of us to come through. Jesus said, if you love me, keep my commandments. He said on another occasion, "Seek ye first the kingdom of God and His righteousness, and all these things shall be added unto you" (Matthew 6:33).

When Solomon became king, he prayed for God to give him the wisdom, the understanding to know how to govern his people. That's why I say to you that the important thing for you to remember is that your first priority must be to abide in that Presence. What really excites me about being a child of God is that God is not way off someplace, that His Spirit is everywhere evenly present. His Spirit abides in me. And if you truly want to know where you go from here—wherever "here" may be for you—then you will begin by turning within to that ever-abiding Presence.

And, you know, the Scriptures also tell us, "Greater is He that is in you than he that is in the world" (1 John 4:4), meaning, in this case, that it's only through the goodness of God that you have achieved whatever you have anyway. So if you will practice every day making that union, making that connection, making that oneness with the presence and power of God that is within you, you'll never again have to raise the question, "Where do I go from here?" You'll get into a trusting attitude and you'll just know that all you have to do is take one day at a time and God will direct your steps. The Scriptures say, trust in Him. Don't depend solely on your human understanding; don't get caught up in the assurance of having a degree. I have mine too, but that degree doesn't mean a hill of beans unless I know the Source, the Intelligence, that I used to earn it.

That's why we have to be very careful in our pursuit of wealth. We get so tied to it, so involved in it that we forget the source. The young man in the parable had truly forgotten the source of his wealth. Jesus spoke to him so beautifully. And those same words are being spoken to you and to me today. Trust in God. Let me go back to that verse, because that's the key: *"Children, how hard is it for them that trust in riches to enter into the kingdom of God."* Trust in God first.

When you wake up, begin the day by saying, "Father-Mother God, it's Your day. You've given it to me to use. Let me begin my day with You." Perhaps you won't get a direct response right away; sometimes you just get a sense of peace, a knowingness that all is well. And then as you go to work and face decisions, quickly go within and ask God for guidance. On days when my desk is piled with work, I pause a few moments before I touch anything, and I say, "Show me where to start." And a thought will come through. I'll look at the pile and I'll know exactly where to begin. And this is true not just of the work I do at my desk, but of whatever I do, wherever I'm going. I always take that time to say, "Father-Mother God, show me."

This method will work for you too. When you pray, just say in the simplest way, "Lord, I love You so much. I love Your presence, Your power in me." Then you will know that everything you do will be in divine order, because the Spirit of the living God is moving through you, speaking through you, guiding you in all things.

This is the basis of our being children of God. We simply have to go back to our Father and ask for direction. So when you ask yourself, "Where do I go from here?" stop and recognize that you haven't accomplished it all. You're going from glory to glory. You're moving step by step toward your perfection. You haven't reached it yet; true perfection is to trust totally in Spirit; true perfection is to be balanced, to use the intellect but to allow it to be spiritualized by the presence of the living God. To help you on your journey, take the following affirmations with you.

AFFIRMATIONS

1. *I abide in the Father, and all my activity is spiritually motivated.*
2. *I know what to do, how to do it, and when to do it.*
3. *Whatever I begin with God will turn out all right.*
4. *Today is the day I put aside all that worried or upset me yesterday.*
5. *I am filled with self-confidence, and with the blessed assurance that I am the master of my life.*
6. *I will succeed, for God is with me and the spirit in me is my inspiration and my capability.*
7. *I know that neither my happiness nor my success depends on any person, place, or thing.*
8. *I am receiving all the good God has for me.*
9. *The peace of Jesus Christ is poured out upon me now and I am relaxed in mind and body.*
10. *Divine order is now established in my mind, body, and affairs.*
11. *God is good all the time, under all circumstances, and in all places.*

Afterword

*I*n chapter one, I promised that this book would show you how to transform your life for the better by practicing the presence of God. I pray that as you have been reading the book and using the affirmations, you have indeed found some aspects of your life changing for the better. As you return to these pages to study parts of the book more carefully, I am confident that you will continue to experience that transformation for the better.

Now I must give you a warning: **You must continue working at this transformation process if you expect those changes to be permanent and if you expect to see other beneficial changes in your life.**

This is not such unusual advice, though. If you have acquired a certain skill—anything from weight lifting to speed reading—whatever it is, you must continually practice it if you expect to retain your ability. The same thing is true of spiritual growth and working personal miracles. You cannot expect to progress if you enter into prayer and affirmations once in a while and forget about this miracle-working power the rest of the time. I have said this repeatedly throughout the book, but I am saying it one more time to emphasize how important it is.

The point of reference in this book has been, from page one, following the example of Jesus as a way of tuning in to God and your God-self. Why? Because *God is all there is; there is nothing else.* To get a sense of how strongly I believe that—and of how strongly I recommend God to you—recall the many references to the Bible that occur in this book.

Truly, the Bible is our source of inspiration, of guidance, and of right thinking. The answers we seek are within those sacred pages. The more time we spend studying the Bible, the more we take into our consciousness the wisdom contained in the Scriptures. Therefore, as another way of making use of this book, I invite you to become especially familiar with the Bible passages cited in these pages, and with their practical application, as an avenue to your own spiritual unfoldment.

Finally, you may have noticed that as the book progresses, affirmations become increasingly dependent upon your own conscious application of the principles. In order to live in the fullness of the moment, you must be able to "pray on your feet." The saying is actually "think on your feet," meaning that in any situation, someone who could think on his feet could quickly determine a reasonable course of action.

"Thinking on your feet" or "praying on your feet" both fall into the category of what we at Hillside call *making religion practical*. Our religion should be a kind that goes on the job with us, to the bank, on the highway, overseas, away to school. Religion is a way of life. Wherever we are, God is. In the same way, *wherever we are, we should have instant access to our spiritual tools*.

The way to develop this kind of instant access, the "praying on your feet," is by practicing the presence of God so often that the awareness of God's presence becomes a part of our conscious thought process.

How long will this "transformation" take? That's entirely up to you. One thing is for sure: the sooner you start, the sooner you eventually will be there.

God loves you, God blesses you, and God appreciates you. And so do I.

About the Author

by
Marion Delaney-Harris
Consultant to Dr. King

The Reverend Dr. Barbara Lewis King has been called one of the most influential spiritual leaders in the world. At the age of thirteen she knew she wanted to be a minister, and her carefully guided paths eventually led her there.

Overcoming a life-threatening physical condition as a teenager, Barbara was inspired to live by increasing her faith in God in her to heal any condition. This faith, this prayer, this vision became the cornerstone by which Barbara was able to build her life's work. She holds a bachelor's degree in sociology, a master's degree and certification in social work, several honorary doctorates in divinity, and a number of years of training in religion and the ministry. She has completed coursework toward a doctorate in educational administration.

Barbara has been an educational administrator, a college teacher, director of the largest merger of three settlement houses in Chicago, and a college dean. She proudly notes that all of these prepared her for the ministry.

She is a native of Houston, Texas, a former resident of Chicago, and now of Atlanta—all claim her as their own because of the impressive and positive impact she makes wherever she lives and works. She is sought throughout the United States to speak, preach, and teach and has been the guest of governments in a number of countries in South Africa, Europe, the Middle East, and the West Indies.

She is an active community leader who serves on a number of boards and commissions as both a gubernatorial and mayoral appointee. Barbara even wears a badge—having been appointed as a chaplain with the local police department and having been sworn in as a captain by the county sheriff.

Barbara combines all of this background into her full-time position as a minister since founding Hillside in 1971. She serves as Chief Executive Officer and member of the Board of Trustees at Hillside, and is the Founder and President of the Barbara King School of Ministry.

Reverend King's dream for Hillside is manifesting annually. This independent church is an ecumenical ministry, a new thinking church, founded on the teachings of Jesus Christ and the practical application of His Principles to everyday living. So popular and necessary are Barbara's messages, sermons, classes, and programs at Hillside, that the original facility was expanded in 1991 to include a 1200-seat "Church-in-the-Round" to accommodate the ever-widening circle of members and friends who are uplifted by her ministry.

Barbara's messages in sermon, song, and books reflect the common theme that WITH GOD, ALL THINGS ARE POSSIBLE! Her life is a testimony; her church is a testimony; her work throughout the world is a testimony; this book is a testimony. Her family is a testimony—Barbara is the mother of a son, Michael, with whom she shares a close relationship and who has been with her throughout the development of her ministry.

Barbara, often fondly called "Dr. Barbara," is someone special, someone who has a lingering presence, a comforting smile, a healing hand, a gentle touch. To so many, she is a minister, a teacher, a businesswoman, a counselor, a queen and king, a mother, a spiritual leader, a grandmommy, a friend. That's why you hear it said, over and over again, that

"She is in stride with the upper progressive movement
of life, and the mark of success is upon her right now!
Thank you, Father-Mother god!
And so it is!"